ESSENTIALS of Financial Analysis

George T. Friedlob
Lydia L.F. Schleifer

John Wiley & Sons, Inc.

Published by John Wiley & Sons, Inc., Hoboken, New Jersey.
Published simultaneously in Canada

Library of Congress Cataloging-in-Publication Data:

Friedlob, G. Thomas.
Essentials of financial analysis / George T. Friedlob, Lydia L. F. Schleifer.
p. cm.—(Essentials series)
Includes bibliographical references and index.
ISBN 0-471-22830-3 (pbk. : alk. paper)
1. Financial statements. 2. Corporation reports. 3. Financial statements—United States. 4. Corporation reports—United States. I. Schleifer, Lydia L. F. (Lydia Lancaster Folger), 1955- II. Title. III. Series.
HG4028.B2 F75 2003
332.63'2042—dc21

2002012427

Printed in the United States of America

10 9 8 7 6 5 4

Contents

Preface

The financial analysis of companies is usually undertaken so that investors, creditors, and other stakeholders can make decisions about those companies. The focus of this book is on the financial analysis of companies that are publicly traded and therefore make public the data and information needed by stakeholders, who can then use the analytical procedures included in this book.

The primary objectives in this book are to

- Provide an overview of financial statements and where and how to obtain them.
- Explain how to use the information provided in annual reports and Securities and Exchange Commission (SEC) filings, to examine a company's profitability, liquidity, and solvency.
- Examine various techniques for evaluating the market value of companies based on their financial reports and stock prices.
- Discuss issues related to the quality of earnings and financial reporting.
- Describe several ways of examining the cash flows of companies.
- Describe new developments in areas like pro forma reporting, economic value added (EVA), and discounted cash flow methods.

Chapter 1 starts by looking briefly at how accounting for resources began. Then, an example of a set of financial statements (for Coca-Cola Company) is included and their content explained. Following that is a comparison of cash-basis and accrual-basis accounting.

Chapter 2 looks at profitability from many angles. Profits are reported on the income statement, so we start with a look at the categories of earnings on the income statement. The chapter discusses operating income and comprehensive income and where to find that information. Because revenue recognition is so much in the spotlight lately, the basics of that principle are discussed. Four of the main analytical techniques used by financial analysts are included: return on assets (ROA), return on equity (ROE), earnings per share (EPS), and the price/earnings (P/E) ratio.

Chapter 3 examines the concepts of liquidity and solvency and how to evaluate those attributes for a company. The primary focus is on the balance sheet. However, also included are some cash flow adequacy ratios, since lack of cash flow can force companies to declare bankruptcy. The chapter discusses how leverage can affect a company. Also included is a discussion of the auditor's decision process when evaluating going concern status. Finally, we include a demonstration of the use of Altman's Z score.

Chapter 4 examines the activity, effectiveness, and productivity measures that can be used to evaluate companies. The chapter discusses several turnover ratios, like accounts receivable and inventory turnover. It also discusses a method of analyzing capacity usage and how to calculate operating leverage and examine its impact on profitability.

Chapter 5 discusses the issue of quality of earnings and how certain aspects of financial reporting enhance or detract from that quality. Because quality is related to how predictive of cash flows the information is, the chapter also includes several cash flow ratios and what information they provide. Common-size cash flow statements take the cash flow analysis one step further. Common-size income statements and balance sheets are also included.

Chapters 6 and 7 discuss relatively recent developments in financial analysis. Chapter 6 includes pro forma reporting and EVA. Chapter 7 discusses e-business and includes several methods for analyzing the value of Internet businesses.

As more and more people make the decision to control their own investment decisions, the need for explanations of financial analysis tools becomes greater. The intent of this book is to provide helpful explanatory information to financial statement users and company stakeholders of all sorts. If you are one of these stakeholders, we hope that this book will help you to make good decisions regarding the businesses in which you have or want to have a stake.

Acknowledgments

The authors would like to acknowledge the contribution of Paul Schleifer to this project. They would also like to thank Judy Howarth for her patience throughout the process of writing this book.

CHAPTER 1

Understanding Financial Statements and Annual Reports

After reading this chapter, you will be able to

- Appreciate the history of accounting
- Understand the basics of the financial statements
- Understand cash-basis versus accrual-basis accounting
- Know how to obtain financial statements, Securities and Exchange Commission (SEC) filings, and annual reports
- Identify the main components of an annual report or 10K filing

Investors and owners have struggled with communicating and analyzing financial performance for centuries. Since the beginning of business activity—and with it, delegation of responsibility—the owner of the invested resources (perhaps a herd of goats) has sought to monitor and evaluate the stewardship of the operating manager (the shepherd). Accounting records have been found in Babylon, Assyria, and Sumeria that date back over 7,000 years. In these early records, scribes described business transactions using wedge-shaped cuneiform writing impressed on clay tablets. For privacy, a tablet was wrapped in a clay sheet, marked with a seal, and fired.

Because there is a natural season to farming and herding, a natural beginning and a natural end, it was easy to analyze the results of activities: The value of the harvest was compared to the value of the seed and other resources, or the growth of the flock was noted after young were born, as in Exhibit 1.1. The same natural beginning and end to business activity was true when ancient sailors such as Columbus or Magellan embarked ventures to find new wealth in faraway places. Early accounting and financial analysis focused on determining the profit from each separate season or venture. Queen Isabella, for example, supplied ships and provisions, and Columbus sailed away. Years later, when he returned, the worth of the New World booty was compared to the cost of the initial provisions. The difference was profit.

Specific ventures, and agriculture and pastoral cycles have natural beginnings and ends. A list of all assets and liabilities was prepared at the beginning and end of the undertaking, and the change was profit or loss. Much the same method is used today, but modern businesses generally have no natural cycle. Barring business failure, modern businesses will go on forever. Plants operate day after day, year after year. Old plants wear out, new plants are built. Even now, some businesses have operated con-

EXHIBIT 1.1

Pastorale Accounting

Size of Herd		
Beginning of spring		50 goats
End of summer		57 goats
Beginning goat herd	50 goats	
Ending goat herd	57 goats	
Increased wealth (profit)		7 goats

tinuously for hundreds of years. Investors, creditors, and others cannot wait for a modern business to naturally wind down before profit is calculated. To solve this problem, the arbitrary cycle of a fiscal year is imposed on business activity.

Many businesses have a busy season and a slow season. Where this is true, businesses may adopt a fiscal, or economic, year that starts and ends in the slow season, rather than using the calendar year with a year end at December 31. For example, Ethan Allen, a furniture manufacturer, and Robert Mondavi, a wine producer, both use a fiscal year that ends on June 30. PriceSmart, a membership shopping club operating in Central America, Asia, and the Caribbean, uses August 31. Net2Phone uses a July 31 year end. Wal-Mart and Kmart have a January 31 year end.

Accounting is the language of business. It is the vehicle for communicating financial information about a company to many different groups of people: managers, owners, creditors, investors, customers, suppliers, government agencies, economists, and others. Each of these groups may have different uses for the information. Owners are concerned that the company produce a profit and increase their wealth. Creditors want to know that the company is liquid enough to make debt payments and solvent enough to repay the loan principle if the business fails. Managers want to be compensated for their work and have confidence their employer will provide job security. Customers and suppliers want to benefit from their ongoing business relationships. The government wants to ensure the public good, by collecting taxes and improving financial reporting. All these stakeholders can benefit and achieve their objectives if they have good accounting information.

Accounting is an ever-changing communicative system. All parties with a stake in the economic environment, upon which accounting reports, continually press for improvements in the information that accounting systems provide. This book presents many traditional as well as new ways of examining financial information that will facilitate the

IN THE REAL WORLD

Opaqueness versus Transparency

The events surrounding Enron's catastrophic bankruptcy have increased the focus on financial reporting by many companies. There has been much discussion on the issue of opaqueness versus transparency, which alludes to whether financial reporting actually is informative enough for decision makers. A lot of pressure has been brought to bear on companies to make their financial statements more transparent. For example, IBM had not disclosed that certain gains on sales of assets had been used to reduce the operating expenses on the income statement. After experiencing a stock price decline that resulted when the *New York Times* reported that IBM's "fourth-quarter earnings met expectations only because of a gain . . . from the sale of its optical transceiver business . . .", IBM decided to improve and increase its financial disclosures. However, John Joyce, IBM's chief financial officer (CFO), disagrees that such gains should be separately disclosed even though he is willing to disclose information about how IBM calculates its operating expenses. So, the push for transparency may result in more information in the notes to the financial statements even if not a change in the amounts on the financial statements themselves.

Source: "IBM Plans to Expand Earnings Reports to Include More Details about Its Income," *The Wall Street Journal*, February 19, 2002.

user's making effective decisions. This chapter provides an overall view of the information typically provided in financial statements.

A Tour of the Financial Statements

We chose the financial statements of The Coca-Cola Company because they show the basics very well and because practically everyone has heard of Coke. The company includes four financial statements in its annual report, and they are shown in Exhibit 1.2. The names of the financial statements are

- Consolidated Statements of Income
- Consolidated Balance Sheets
- Consolidated Statements of Cash Flows
- Consolidated Statements of Share-Owners' Equity

Notice that the balance sheet covers two years and the other statements cover three years. All the titles listed above include the word "consolidated" because the statements include the accounts of The Coca-Cola Company (Coca-Cola) and all subsidiaries in which the company's ownership interest enables it to exert control. A starting point for determin-

EXHIBIT 1.2

The Coca-Cola Company and Subsidiaries

Consolidated Statements of Income

Year Ended December 31,	**2001**	**2000**	**1999**
	(in millions, except per share data)		
NET OPERATING REVENUES	$20,092	$19,889	$19,284
Cost of goods sold	6,044	6,204	6,009
GROSS PROFIT	14,048	13,685	13,275
Selling, administrative and general expenses	8,696	8,551	8,480
Other operating charges	—	1,443	813
OPERATING INCOME	5,352	3,691	3,982
Interest income	325	345	260
Interest expense	289	447	337

EXHIBIT 1.2

THE COCA-COLA COMPANY AND SUBSIDIARIES CONTINUED

Year Ended December 31,	2001	2000	1999
Equity income (loss)	152	(289)	(184)
Other income—net	39	99	98
Gains on issuances of stock by equity investees	91	—	—
INCOME BEFORE INCOME TAXES AND CUMULATIVE EFFECT OF ACCOUNTING CHANGE	5,670	3,399	3,819
Income taxes	1,691	1,222	1,388
INCOME BEFORE CUMULATIVE EFFECT OF ACCOUNTING CHANGE	3,979	2,177	2,431
Cumulative effect of accounting change, net of income taxes	(10)	—	—
NET INCOME	$ 3,969	$ 2,177	$ 2,431
BASIC NET INCOME PER SHARE			
Before accounting change	$ 1.60	$ .88	$ .98
Cumulative effect of accounting change	—	—	—
	$ 1.60	$ .88	$ .98
DILUTED NET INCOME PER SHARE			
Before accounting change	$ 1.60	$ .88	$ .98
Cumulative effect of accounting change	—	—	—
	$ 1.60	$ .88	$ .98
AVERAGE SHARES OUTSTANDING	2,487	2,477	2,469
Dilutive effect of stock options	—	10	18
AVERAGE SHARES OUTSTANDING ASSUMING DILUTION	2,487	2,487	2,487

EXHIBIT 1.2

THE COCA-COLA COMPANY AND SUBSIDIARIES CONTINUED

Consolidated Balance Sheets

December 31,	**2001**	**2000**
	(in millions except share data)	
ASSETS		
CURRENT		
Cash and cash equivalents	$ 1,866	$ 1,819
Marketable securities	68	73
	1,934	1,892
Trade accounts receivable, less allowances of $59 in 2001 and $62 in 2000	1,882	1,757
Inventories	1,055	1,066
Prepaid expenses and other assets	2,300	1,905
TOTAL CURRENT ASSETS	7,171	6,620
INVESTMENTS AND OTHER ASSETS		
Equity method investments		
Coca-Cola Enterprises Inc.	788	707
Coca-Cola Amatil Limited	432	617
Coca-Cola HBC S.A.	791	758
Other, principally bottling companies	3,117	3,164
Cost method investments, principally bottling companies	294	519
Other assets	2,792	2,364
	8,214	8,129
PROPERTY, PLANT AND EQUIPMENT		
Land	217	225
Buildings and improvements	1,812	1,642
Machinery and equipment	4,881	4,547
Containers	195	200
	7,105	6,614
Less allowances for depreciation	2,652	2,446

EXHIBIT 1.2

THE COCA-COLA COMPANY AND SUBSIDIARIES CONTINUED

December 31,	2001	2000
	4,453	4,168
TRADEMARKS AND OTHER INTANGIBLE ASSETS	2,579	1,917
	$ 22,417	$ 20,834
LIABILITIES AND SHARE-OWNERS' EQUITY		
CURRENT		
Accounts payable and accrued expenses	$ 3,679	$ 3,905
Loans and notes payable	3,743	4,795
Current maturities of long-term debt	156	21
Accrued income taxes	851	600
TOTAL CURRENT LIABILITIES	8,429	9,321
LONG-TERM DEBT	1,219	835
OTHER LIABILITIES	961	1,004
DEFERRED INCOME TAXES	442	358
SHARE-OWNERS' EQUITY		
Common stock, $.25 par value		
Authorized: 5,600,000,000 shares		
Issued: 3,491,465,016 shares in 2001;		
3,481,882,834 shares in 2000	873	870
Capital surplus	3,520	3,196
Reinvested earnings	23,443	21,265
Accumulated other comprehensive income		
and unearned compensation on restricted		
stock	(2,788)	(2,722)
	25,048	22,609

EXHIBIT 1.2

THE COCA-COLA COMPANY AND SUBSIDIARIES CONTINUED

December 31,	2001	2000
Less treasury stock, at cost (1,005,237,693 shares in 2001; 997,121,427 shares in 2000)	13,682	13,293
	11,366	9,316
	$ 22,417	$ 20,834

Consolidated Statements of Cash Flows

Year Ended December 31,	2001	2000	1999
			(in millions)
OPERATING ACTIVITIES			
Net income	$ 3,969	$ 2,177	$ 2,431
Depreciation and amortization	803	773	792
Deferred income taxes	56	3	97
Equity income or loss, net of dividends	(54)	380	292
Foreign currency adjustments	(60)	196	(41)
Gains on issuances of stock by equity investees	(91)	—	—
Gains on sales of assets, including bottling interests	(85)	(127)	(49)
Other operating charges	—	916	799
Other items	34	119	119
Net change in operating assets and liabilities	(462)	(852)	(557)
Net cash provided by operating activities	4,110	3,585	3,883

EXHIBIT 1.2

THE COCA-COLA COMPANY AND SUBSIDIARIES CONTINUED

Year Ended December 31,	2001	2000	1999
INVESTING ACTIVITIES			
Acquisitions and investments, principally trademarks and bottling companies	(651)	(397)	(1,876)
Purchases of investments and other assets	(456)	(508)	(518)
Proceeds from disposals of investments and other assets	455	290	176
Purchases of property, plant and equipment	(769)	(733)	(1,069)
Proceeds from disposals of property, plant and equipment	91	45	45
Other investing activities	142	138	(179)
Net cash used in investing activities	(1,188)	(1,165)	(3,421)
FINANCING ACTIVITIES			
Issuances of debt	3,011	3,671	3,411
Payments of debt	(3,937)	(4,256)	(2,455)
Issuances of stock	164	331	168
Purchases of stock for treasury	(277)	(133)	(15)
Dividends	(1,791)	(1,685)	(1,580)
Net cash used in financing activities	(2,830)	(2,072)	(471)
EFFECT OF EXCHANGE RATE CHANGES ON CASH AND CASH EQUIVALENTS	(45)	(140)	(28)
CASH AND CASH EQUIVALENTS			
Net increase (decrease) during the year	47	208	(37)
Balance at beginning of year	1,819	1,611	1,648
Balance at end of year	$ 1,866	$ 1,819	$ 1,611

ing control is when a company owns more than 50 percent of the voting stock of another company. Coca-Cola states in its "Management's Discussion and Analysis" (MD&A) that "all majority-owned entities in which our Company's control is considered other than temporary are consolidated."

Starting with the income statement, the next section will give a brief explanation of each line item.

Income Statement

- *Net operating revenues.* Revenues earned performing fundamental business operations. Coca-Cola's revenue recognition policy is to record revenue "when title passes to our bottling partners or our customers."
- *Cost of goods sold.* The cost of the inventory that Coca-Cola sold to its bottling partners or customers
- *Gross profit.* The difference between sales (or operating) revenues and cost of goods sold
- *Selling, administrative, and general expenses.* Operating expenses in addition to cost of goods sold. The bulk of this category goes to marketing and advertising for Coca-Cola.
- *Other operating charges.* A category that may include nonrecurring expenses and costs like write-downs of asset values and settlements of lawsuits
- *Operating income.* Typically is the income from basic business operations and is also known as earnings before interest and taxes. For Coca-Cola, this is also before inclusion of items related to investments that Coca-Cola has made in other companies.
- *Interest income and interest expense.* Interest earned on investments and interest incurred for borrowing, like commercial paper debt

- *Equity income or loss.* This is Coca-Cola's share of the income earned by companies that Coca-Cola has bought enough stock in to be able to influence their management practices.
- *Other income.* Can include atypical events like when a subsidiary merges with another company and decreases the parent's (i.e., Coca-Cola's) ownership interest in the combined activity.
- *Gains on issuances of stock by equity investees.* An equity investee is a company that Coca-Cola owns stock in. The investee issued more stock to a third party, Coca-Cola's investment value increased, so Coca-Cola had a gain.
- *Income taxes.* The income tax effect of every item preceding this line
- *Income before cumulative effect of accounting change.* Also known as income from continuing operations; operations that are discontinued or are being discontinued are shown separately
- *Cumulative effect of accounting change, net of income taxes.* When a company changes how it accounts for something, it may be necessary to report the impact on net income in prior years as if the company had always used the new method. In Coca-Cola's case, the company adapted a new requirement for reporting derivatives and hedging activities.
- *Net income.* The "bottom line"!
- *Basic net income per share.* Commonly known as earnings per share (EPS). This is net income divided by the average number of common shares outstanding (a company may disclose the number of shares here, as Coca-Cola does, or in the notes)
- *Diluted net income per share.* Reported only if not greater than basic EPS. Diluted EPS shows how much reduction would occur if additional common shares were issued through conversion of other securities or exercise of stock options.

Balance Sheet

- *Assets.* Resources that a company has legal control of
- *Current assets.* Cash and other assets likely to be converted to cash or consumed within a year; usually includes the following five components
    1. *Cash and cash equivalents.* The latter are marketable and highly liquid securities with short-term maturities (say, no more than three months). May include CDs and money market funds
    2. *Marketable securities.* May include any investment in the stocks or bonds of another entity (probably small enough to not involve influence or control)
    3. *Trade accounts receivable.* Receivables that result from credit sales to customers, reduced by an amount that is likely to be uncollectible
    4. *Inventories.* Contains merchandise inventory for a retail company; raw materials, supplies, work-in-process, and finished goods inventories for a manufacturing company. Companies disclose in the notes what inventory method(s) are used (e.g., first-in, first-out [FIFO] or last-in, first-out [LIFO] or average)
    5. *Prepaid expenses and other assets.* Includes resources paid for but not consumed yet, like prepaid rent, prepaid insurance, prepaid advertising, and supplies
- *Equity method investments.* For Coca-Cola, this includes "investments in companies in which we have the ability to exercise significant influence [traditionally 20%–50%] over operating and financial policies, including certain investments where there is a temporary majority interest." The equity method involves recognizing a share of the net earnings of investee companies (subsidiaries) in the income of the investor (Coca-Cola)

- *Cost method investments.* These are also investments in other companies but of a lesser percentage so as not to have influence (less than 20 percent). These investments are carried at cost or fair market value.
- *Other assets.* For Coca-Cola, this includes investments in infrastructure programs with bottlers and advance payments to customers for distribution rights; in general, this category contains all assets that do not fit into the other categories.
- *Property, plant and equipment.* Typically, tangible, long-term plant assets (useful for more than a year); some plant assets (not land) are depreciated.
- *Trademarks and other intangible assets.* May also include patents, copyrights, goodwill, and other resources that have no physical existence.
- *Liabilities and share-owners' equity.* Represent the sources of all those assets on the other side of the balance sheet (e.g., the sources being either creditors [liabilities] or owners [owners' equity])
- *Current liabilities.* Obligations that will be settled within a year, usually, by payment from current assets
- *Accounts payable and accrued expenses.* Obligations to parties that have provided goods or services to the company. May include liabilities for purchases, wages and salaries, taxes, and advertising
- *Loans and notes payable.* If current, probably includes commercial paper from banks in the United States and outstanding amounts from a line of credit
- *Current maturities of long-term debt.* The portion of a company's long-term debt (typically, notes and bonds) that is due in the coming year
- *Accrued income taxes.* Taxes associated with profits already earned but on which the payment is avoided in the current year
- *Long-term debt.* Includes interest-bearing debt that is due beyond a year (typically, notes and bonds)

- *Deferred income taxes.* Deferred taxes can arise when the tax expense (based on accounting income) is different from the taxes payable (based on taxable income); accounting income can differ significantly from taxable income.
- *Share-owners' equity.* Represents the property of owners; the amount of the assets that owners have claim to
- *Common stock.* The total par value of common stock issued to date
- *Capital surplus.* The amount of the proceeds, received from original stock issuances, in excess of the par value (i.e., by the end of 2001 Coca-Cola had received $4,393 million from issuing common stock made up of $873 million par value plus $3,520 million excess). Par value and excess (or surplus) together represent the contributed capital (contributed by owners).
- *Reinvested earnings.* The cumulative amount of net income reinvested in the company (also called *retained earnings*) after any dividends have been distributed to owners
- *Accumulated other comprehensive income, etc.* Includes other changes in shareholders' equity that are *not* on the income statement and *not* a result of transactions with owners in their capacity as owners (this component is discussed further in Chapter 2)
- *Treasury stock.* Represents the cost incurred by a company in buying back its own, formerly outstanding, stock

Cash Flow Statement

- *Operating activities.* Activities related to the fundamental business operation of the company (i.e., buying and selling goods and/or services)
- *Net income.* When the operating section of the cash flow statement begins with net income, then it has been prepared by reconciling net income to cash provided by operating activities.

- *Depreciation and amortization.* These noncash expenses reduce net income but do not affect cash, so they are added back to net income in order to arrive at cash from operations.
- *Net change in operating assets and liabilities.* For Coca-Cola this net change is explained in a note.

  In general, the adjustments explained in the note are related to increases and decreases in current assets and current liabilities (here called operating assets and liabilities). To explain just one of those changes, let's think about credit sales. Credit sales increase sales revenues (and therefore increase net income) but do not affect cash (the company receives an account receivable instead of getting cash), so the increase in accounts receivable should be deducted from net income to arrive at cash from operations.
- *Investing activities.* Activities generally related to the purchase and sale of long-term assets. Coca-Cola bought and sold various property, plant and equipment assets and acquired bottling companies and trademarks.
- *Financing activities.* Activities generally related to obtaining financial resources from the credit market and stock market (or paying off debt or paying dividends)
- *Effect of exchange rate changes on cash and cash equivalents.* Because Coca-Cola operates in a global environment, it is exposed to the risk of changes in foreign currency exchange rates. To reduce this risk, the company engages in foreign currency hedging. These hedging activities are described in the notes.

Share-owners' Equity Statement

The format of this statement looks complicated, but it basically is formatted to show all the changes in all the equity accounts over a three-year period. One year picks up where the previous year leaves off. The section on the year 2001 follows.

- *Comprehensive income.* Changes in share-owners' equity that are not part of net income or due to transactions with owners
- *Net income.* The amount of income as shown on the income statement. Notice that it is added to reinvested earnings (see also *dividends*, the last component in this list).
- *Translation adjustments.* Contains the dollar effect of changes in foreign currency exchange rates
- *Cumulative effect of SFAS No. 133.* Shows the effect of adapting Statement of Financial Accounting Standards (SFAS) No. 133 on January 1, 2001. This SFAS requires companies to show the fair value of derivative instruments as either assets or liabilities on the balance sheet. Derivative instruments are generally used to reduce exposure to risk.
- *Net gain (loss) on derivatives.* Contains gains and losses on hedges. Derivative instruments are supposed to be classified as a fair-value hedge, a cash-flow hedge, or a hedge of net investment in a foreign operation (depending on the exposure being hedged). For Coca-Cola, the $92 reported here is mostly related to a foreign currency cash-flow hedge.
- *Net change in unrealized gain (loss) on securities.* This contains the effect of a changing fair market value for securities classified as available for sale
- *Minimum pension liability.* This represents, in Coca-Cola's case, a decrease in comprehensive income due to having to increase a liability related to pension plans.
- *Stock issued to employees exercising stock options.* Represents the cash raised by selling stock to employees at a specified option price
- *Restricted stock.* Restricted stock plans are for certain officers and key employees of the company. These are adjustments to equity accounts that may or may not have affected the income statement, but did not directly result in a cash flow.

TIPS & TECHNIQUES

Financial Performance Measurement Project

At press time, the most recent update on the Financial Accounting Standards Board's (FASB) Web site pertaining to its financial performance project read, in part, as follows:

> **Project Objectives**
>
> The primary objectives of the project are (1) to improve the quality of information displayed in financial statements so that investors, creditors, and others can better evaluate an enterprise's financial performance and (2) to ascertain that sufficient information is contained in the financial statements to permit calculation of key financial measures used by investors and creditors. Several of the respondents to the August Proposal suggested that this project, although limited to the display of items and measures in financial statements, is especially timely because the proliferation of alternative and inconsistent financial performance measures is undermining high-quality financial reporting, which is essential to well-informed investment decisions and efficient capital markets.
>
> The project will focus on form and content, classification and aggregation, and display of specified items and summarized amounts on the face of all basic financial statements, interim as well as annual. That includes determining whether to require the display of certain items determined to be key measures or necessary for the calculation of key measures. The project will not address management discussion and analysis or the reporting of so-called pro forma earnings in press releases or other communications outside financial statements and does not include segment information or matters of recognition or measurement of items in financial statements.

The outcome of this project might be right around the corner. Go to *www.fasb.org* to find out what changes may occur and when.

    - Tax benefit from employees' stock option and restricted stock plans
    - Restricted stock and other stocks plans, less cancellations
    - Amortization of restricted stock
    - Unearned restricted stock adjustment
- *Purchase of stock for the treasury.* Represents payment to existing stockholders to buy back their Coca-Cola stock
- *Dividends.* Payments to shareholders (the only other thing, besides net income, to affect Reinvested Earnings)

IN THE REAL WORLD

Changes in GAAP

If earnings appear to improve from one period to the next, it may not necessarily reflect better success in operations. Sometimes earnings are affected by a change in the accounting methods a company uses or a change in what generally accepted accounting principles (GAAP) or the SEC will allow. For example, the oil industry will be affected by a change that the SEC allowed in February 2002. Before February, energy companies had to recognize the full decline of the price of gas as a charge against earnings. In February, the SEC allowed Houston Exploration Company to reduce that charge by the benefit gained from a cash flow hedge. For example, if the price of gas goes from $2.00 to $1.00 per gallon but a hedge agreement guarantees the company will receive no less than $1.50, then the charge against earnings will be at $.50 per gallon rather than the full decline of $1.00. As a result, earnings are higher after the new accounting guidance but the cash flow itself is not affected. The lesson is: Take good news (higher earnings) with a grain of salt.

Source: "Accounting Change May Boost Earnings at Oil Firms if Hedging Gains Are Figured," *The Wall Street Journal*, March 20, 2002.

A Quick Review of Cash-Basis versus Accrual-Basis Accounting

The balance sheet is given its name because the left and right sides balance each other. Assets on the left should always equal the sum of the liabilities and owners' equity on the right

$$\text{Assets} = \text{Liabilities} + \text{Owners' equity}$$

Furthermore, owners' equity contains the retained earnings balance that accumulates by adding the net income to it at the end of every period. So the accounting equation shown above can be expanded as follows:

IN THE REAL WORLD

The Importance of Notes to the Financial Statements

One aspect of financial analysis should include a study of what short sellers look at in their decision making. Short selling involves borrowing stock to sell when its price is high and buying it back to return it when its price is lower. The short seller benefits from the decline of stock value. Examining what makes a short seller pessimistic about a company can be a valuable tool. For example, short seller James Chanos was alerted by a fairly complicated-sounding note entitled "Related Party Transactions," which mentioned that an Enron officer was a "managing member" of another company with which Enron had engaged in transactions. Related-party transactions, especially if they are not clearly disclosed, could make one wonder if there are conflicts of interest wherein the company itself is not being well served and the substance of transactions may not be what they seem.

Source: "Enron Short Seller Detected Red Flags in Regulatory Filings," *The Wall Street Journal*, November 5, 2001, C1.

Cash + Other assets = Liabilities + Owners' equity + Revenues − Expenses

Basing a spreadsheet on the above equation (notice that assets are split into cash and other assets) helps to show how the traditional accounting system has come to be known as a double-entry system (it is like Newton's Third Law of Motion, which says that every action must have an equal and opposite reaction). The following spreadsheet shows many possible ways to affect an accounting system and still balance.

We are assuming that cash must be involved in order to show what transactions can possibly be entered in a cash-basis-only system (see Exhibit 1.3).

IN THE REAL WORLD

Write-Offs

The traditional approach to write-offs was to get them out in the open, then ignore them, and even sometimes watch the company's stock price go up—figuring that the worst was over. Research has shown that this may no longer be appropriate. Write-offs in 2001 for companies in the Standard & Poor's 500 stock index totaled more than in the previous half decade. Simultaneously, bankruptcies increased. Multex.com and *The Wall Street Journal* examined statistics for 1996–2001 for public companies with market capitalization of at least $1 billion and found that the group with the largest charges relative to revenue saw their stock prices decline by 9.4 percent within 90 days. Companies with the smallest charges had a median gain of 1.48 percent. According to Marc Gerstein, director of investment research at Multex.com, "If you want to weed out stocks to look at for investment purposes, companies with unusually large write-offs are a good place to start."

Source: "Stock Gurus Disregard Most Big Write-offs, but They Often Hold Vital Clues to Outlook," *The Wall Street Journal*, December 31, 2001.

EXHIBIT 1.3

Cash-Basis Accounting

	Balance Sheet				Income Statement	
	Cash +	**Other Assets =**	**Liabilities +**	**Owners' Equity +**	**Revenue –**	**Expenses**
1.	+	–				
2.	+		+			
3.	+			+		
4.	+				+	
5.	–					–
6.	–			–		
7.	–		–			
8.	–	+				

Examples of explanations for the transactions include:

1. If cash increases and another asset decreases, the transaction could have been a sale of equipment for cash.
2. An increase in both cash and a liability could signify that the company borrowed money from the bank or received payment for work contracted to be performed later.
3. An increase in cash and owners' equity would result from a company issuing its stock to investors.
4. An increase in cash and revenues would result from a cash sale to a customer.
5. A decrease in cash and also in the expense column (which really means that expenses increased) would result if a company paid its rent for the month.
6. A decrease in cash and in owners' equity results when a company pays out cash dividends.

7. A decrease in cash and liabilities results when a company pays off debt.

8. A decrease in cash and an increase in other assets results when a company buys inventory to hold for sale later.

Now, let's examine the transactions that can be recorded under the accrual basis of accounting (see Exhibit 1.4). Notice that none of the following transactions affect cash.

Examples of explanations for the transactions include:

1. Noncash assets could increase and liabilities increase if a company enters into a long-term capital lease of, for example, equipment.

EXHIBIT 1.4

Accrual-Basis Accounting

	Balance Sheet				**Income Statement**	
	Cash +	**Other Assets =**	**Liabilities +**	**Owners' Equity +**	**Revenue –**	**Expenses**
1.		+	+			
2.		+		+		
3.		+			+	
4.		–				–
5.		–			–	
6.			+			–
7.			+	–		
8.			–	+		
9.			–		+	
10.				+		–
11.				+ and –		

2. Noncash assets could increase and owners' equity increase if a company issues stock in exchange for land.
3. Noncash assets could increase and revenues increase for a credit sale (the asset would be accounts receivable).

IN THE REAL WORLD

A Tool for Financial Analysis:

XBRL: Extensible Business Reporting Language

- *What is it?* Software that will be added to accounting and financial reporting software so that financial information can be better accessed and used.
- *How does it work?* XBRL code will be used to tag and automatically translate all business information so that the data can be searched, identified, linked, and analyzed.
- *What will it accomplish?* XBRL will enable financial information users to perform fast and accurate searches of business data. They will be able to "tailor the search for multiple companies' data and export [it] easily into a spreadsheet for further analysis; since each piece of information is identified with a tag, comparisons and calculations can be automated."*
- *Who will benefit?* Anyone who prepares or uses business data: organizations, auditors, bankers, shareholders, and investors.

*"Finally, Business Talks the Same Language," *Journal of Accountancy*, August 2000, 24–30.

4. Noncash assets would decrease when they are depreciated and an expense recorded (depreciation expense).

5. Noncash assets decrease and owners' equity decreases when certain investments (classified as available for sale) are written down to market value and the unrealized loss reported as a deduction to owners' equity.

6. A liability (like wages or taxes payable) increases and an expense is recorded (wages or tax expense) when accruals are recorded at the end of an accounting period.

7. A liability increases and owners' equity decreases when a dividend is declared (the dividend does not have to be paid yet to be recorded).

8. A liability is decreased and owners' equity increased when convertible bonds are converted to stocks and the stock issued.

9. A liability decreases and revenues increase when a company performs a service that enables it to earn the payment received some time ago (or when time goes by and the rental payment received last month has now been earned).

10. Owners' equity increases and expenses are recorded if an employee is paid with stock instead of cash for services performed.

11. An increase and decrease occur completely within the owners' equity accounts when a stock dividend is distributed.

Notice that quite a few transactions can affect the income statement (revenues and expenses) without affecting cash at all. So there is a lot of room for judgment since noncash transactions have to be recorded at fair market value and market value can be more or less objectively determinable, depending on the circumstances.

Following are some useful Web sites for obtaining and understanding financial statements.

TIPS AND TECHNIQUES

Beware Companies' Promotion of Their Own Stock

Recent events demonstrate that companies have a vested interest in promoting their own stock and boosting the perceived chances at growth in value. For example, some Enron employees reported that they had been asked to sit in a trading room and make it look like they were busy trading when the financial analysts came through on tour. In addition, some financial analysts report that when they say anything about a company's financial situation that might put that company in a bad light, their access to the company is sometimes affected and former contacts become irate and/or inaccessible. So it is apparent that companies want to look as good as possible.

Financial statement users and analysts should be aware of where this bias may creep into a company's financial reporting. Deanna Burgess has analyzed the graphs in a sample of annual reports and found that about a fifth of them had vertical-scale alterations that have the potential to mislead the reader into thinking that the changes, shown in the data graphed, are more significant than they really are. Vertical scale alterations are present when the origin is something other than zero. It is important to be aware of this because Burgess found that people's perceptions were affected by even the slightest alteration: "Virtually no amount of graphical manipulation was acceptable; any alteration in the vertical scale caused a sizable difference in readers' perceptions."

Source: Deanna Oxender Burgess, "Graphical Sleight of Hand," *Journal of Accountancy*, February 2002, 45–51.

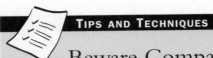

Web Sites for Further Research

Financial Statements—General

- *www.sec.gov*
- *www.freeEdgar.com*
- *www.pwcglobal.com*

Financial Statements—Individual Companies

- The Coca-Cola Company: *www.coca-cola.com*
- Pfizer: *www.pfizer.com*
- The Dow Chemical Company: *www.dow.com*
- Corning Incorporated: *www.corning.com*
- BankOne Corporation: *www.bankone.com*
- General Electric Company: *www.ge.com/annual01*

Industry Averages, Industry Information and Financial Analysis, and Information About Stock Markets

- *http://cbs.marketwatch.com/news*
- *www.usadata.com*—stock quotes, research, and the like
- *www.esignal.com*—stock quotes and the like
- *http://sdsmarketwatch.com*
- *http://invest-faq.com*
- *www.geoinvest.com*—stock market information, free stock research
- *www.nelnet.com*—links to more than 2,700 investment managers from websites worldwide
- *www.dtonline.com*
- *www.1stresearch.com*—industry profiles: overview, trends, and so on

- *www.justquotes.com*—current and historical stock prices and much more
- *www.ibbotson.com*—industry information on cost of capital and risk
- *www.options-iri.com*—provides insights about the market
- *www.oio.com*—stock quotes, volatility charts, market news
- *www.dogsofthedow.com*—stock selection information, stock histories from 1996 to the present
- *www.spglobal.com*
- *www.cnnfn.com*
- *www.dowjones.com*
- *www.nbci.com*
- *www.morningstar.com*—market news, analyst research
- *www.schwab.com*—market news, charts
- *www.smartmoney.com*—quotes, market updates
- *www.fool.com*—investment news, stock quotes and research, and the like
- *www.multex.com*—contains market research
- *http://yahoo.marketguide.com*
- *http://www.financialweb.com*
- *http://moneycentral.msn.com/investor/invsub/results/compare.asp*
- *http://www.corporateinformation.com*

Education

- *www.free-ed.net*
- *http://library.thinkquest.org/3088/*—EduStock.com: Edustock is an educational Web page designed to teach young and old alike what the stock market is and how it can work for them.

- *http://www.investsmart.com.au/home/default.asp*—InvestSmart.com
- *http://TeachMeFinance.com*
- *www.tiaa-cref.org/library/dictionary*—dictionary of financial terms
- *www.financiallearning.com*
- *www.investorguide.com*
- *www.fool.com*—for The Motley Fool

General Business Information and Current Business Events

- *www.wsj.com*
- *www.fortune.com*
- *www.ustoday.com*
- *www.nytimes.com*
- *www.apoline.com*
- *www.reuters.com*

Generally Accepted Accounting Principles (GAAP) and Generally Accepted Auditing Standards (GAAS)

- *www.aicpa.org*
- *www.fasb.org*
- *www.gasb.org*
- *www.cpa2biz.com*

Advice for Advisers

- *www.investmentadvisor.com*

General Knowledge and Background in Financial Matters

- *http://ourworld.compuserve.com/homepages/Bonehead_Finance*
- *www.fool.com*
- *www.bernardsvill.org/invest.htm*
- *http://smartmoney.com*
- *www.ozsoft.com*
- *http://moneycentral.msn.com*
- *www.featuresource.com*—business articles

Search Engines and Sites to Find Other Sites

- *www.yahoo.com*
- *http://lii.org*
- *www.webbieworld.com*—features picks for popular sites in many categories, including business
- *www.google.com*

E-business Sites

- *www.dci.com*—lots of information about information technology
- *www.bcg.com*—look at BCG Publications for information on e-commerce
- *www.website101.com*
- *www.lexmercatoria.org*
- *www.gbd.org*
- *www.zdnet.com/enterprise/e-business*

Summary

Organizations have many ways to communicate information about themselves. Different decision makers have different ideas about what they want to know about an organization. However, when it comes to deciding whether to let an organization use your money, it is the financial information that is most needed. And that financial information comes in many forms. The fortunate thing is that financial reporting does follow GAAP, enabling one to evaluate and compare companies. In addition, there are numerous analytical techniques one can use to gain further insight into what the numbers mean. This book covers many of those traditional analytical techniques as well as some relatively new ones.

CHAPTER 2

Analyzing Profitability

After reading this chapter, you will be able to

- Identify the types of earnings reported in the income statement
- Understand the concept of operating income
- Understand the concept of comprehensive income
- Identify the information revealed in a company's comprehensive income
- Understand the revenue recognition principle
- Evaluate the return on investment (ROI) of a company using financial statements
- Evaluate the return on equity (ROE) of a company using financial statements
- Understand the concept of earnings per share (EPS)
- Examine and understand the price/earnings (P/E) ratio of a company

Analyzing Profitability

Any analysis of profitability would have to begin with a discussion of what profit is, where one can find it reported, and how one can measure it. Profit is viewed as the same thing as net income, which is the bottom-line result on the income statement. Net income is calculated as revenues and gains less expenses and losses. Most of the information on an income statement is related to operations and can be used to assess and understand how the business is performing.

The income statement is an accrual-basis income statement. This means that it contains information about economic activity that did not necessarily result in a cash flow. For example, the sales revenue will most likely contain credit sales as well as cash sales. Sometimes, a company may even report net income on the income statement but negative cash flow from operations on the cash flow statement. The company may, for example, have paid cash for inventory or other resources that will not be consumed and expensed until next year. Or a company may report a net loss on the income statement and a positive cash flow from operations on the cash flow statement. (This is the case with the Dow Chemical Company financial statements that we will examine later in the chapter.)

When companies report their earnings in press releases, they often include, in addition to the dollar amount of the net income, a dollar amount for what net income would be without one-time charges. One-time charges are expenses or costs that, according to the company, do not happen on a regular basis, like restructuring charges or goodwill write-offs. The company is usually trying to focus the reader's attention on what the company views as the normal earnings (which is usually a more optimistic result). Some would criticize this approach by saying that when a company has one-time charges year after year, they become an expected and normal part of the business's financial picture. Be that as it may, the interested financial statement user can get this information in a more complete context in the set of comparative income statements (which typically includes three years) and make a judgment about what happens regularly and what does not. The next section will look briefly at the conceptual background of reporting accounting information, and after that the chapter will look in more detail at the income statement, particularly discussing the types of earnings to be found on the income statement.

Recognition, Measurement, and Reporting

Analyzing the profitability of a company depends on obtaining information about the profit reported by the company. A lot of judgment may go on behind the scenes to reach that number. The Financial Accounting Standards Board (FASB) guides that judgment with its pronouncements (FASB Statements) and a conceptual body of literature known as Statements of Financial Accounting Concepts. The theory in these concept statements provides guidance concerning three main issues related to what amount of profits to report: recognition, measurement, and reporting.[1]

Recognition

Numbers are in the financial statements because someone made a journal entry. The journal entry results when someone decides there is an amount (or several amounts) that must be recorded to represent a transaction. In some cases, many assumptions and estimates must be made to reach that number. When that number is recorded, an economic transaction is *recognized*. The issue of revenue recognition will be discussed further later in the chapter.

Measurement

In order for an economic event to be recognized, it has to be measured. There are five ways to measure an economic event, though not all events have all five attributes:

1. *Historical cost.* The cash equivalent price paid for goods or services on the acquisition date
2. *Current replacement cost.* The price that would be paid currently to purchase or replace equivalent goods or services (e.g., a computer that has declined in value). There are two ways to measure

replacement cost: The replacement of the computer with an identical old computer or the replacement of the computing power the computer contained

3. *Current market value.* The price that would be received from selling an asset (e.g., the market value of an investment in stock may change daily)
4. *Net realizable value.* The amount of cash expected to be received from the sale of an item (e.g., net accounts receivable)
5. *Present (discounted) value.* Future cash flows from the sale or use of an item discounted to their present value at an appropriate interest rate (e.g., the present value of long-term debt is less than its maturity value)

Even if all these values are about the same for an asset when it is purchased, business and environmental conditions may cause these five values to diverge over time. The best way to value items in the financial statements depends on how reliable the information is. For example, information about the market value of an investment in currently traded stock is more reliable than information about the appraised market value of an old building.

Reporting

According to the FASB, companies should provide financial statements to the public that show the following:

- Financial position at the end of the period
- Earnings (net income) for the period
- Cash flows during the period
- Investments by and distributions to owners during the period
- Comprehensive income (total nonowner changes in equity) for the period

The first three are shown on the balance sheet, income statement, and cash flow statement, respectively. The other two may be reported in separate statements of their own or in a stockholders' equity statement. The Dow Chemical Company happens to report all five of the possible financial statements. Exhibits 2.1 through 2.3 show the Consolidated Statements of Income, Consolidated Balance Sheets, and Consolidated Statements of Comprehensive Income.

EXHIBIT 2.1

The Dow Chemical Company and Subsidiaries

Consolidated Statements of Income

For the years ended December 31	2001	2000	1999
	(in millions, except per share amounts)		
Net Sales	$ 27,805	$ 29,534	$ 25,859
Cost of sales	23,652	24,131	20,300
Research and development expenses	1,072	1,119	1,075
Selling, general and administrative expenses	1,765	1,825	1,776
Amortization of intangibles	178	139	160
Purchased in-process research and development charges	69	6	6
Special charges	–	–	94
Merger-related expenses and restructuring	1,487	–	–
Insurance and finance company operations, pretax income	30	85	150
Equity in earnings of nonconsolidated affiliates	29	354	95
Sundry income—net	394	352	329

EXHIBIT 2.1

THE DOW CHEMICAL COMPANY AND SUBSIDIARIES

For the years ended December 31	2001	2000	1999
Earnings before Interest, Income Taxes, and Minority Interests	35	3,105	3,022
Interest income	85	146	132
Interest expense and amortization of debt discount	733	665	564
Income (Loss) before Income Taxes and Minority Interests	(613)	2,586	2,590
Provision (Credit) for income taxes	(228)	839	874
Minority interests' share in income	32	72	74
Preferred stock dividends	–	–	5
Income (Loss) before Cumulative Effect of Change in Accounting Principle	(417)	1,675	1,637
Cumulative effect of change in accounting principle	32	–	(20)
Net Income (Loss) Available for Common Stockholders	$ (385)	$ 1,675	$ 1,617
Share Data			
Earnings (Loss) before cumulative effect of change in accounting principle per common share—basic	$ (0.46)	$ 1.88	$ 1.87
Earnings (Loss) per common share—basic	$ (0.43)	$ 1.88	$ 1.85
Earnings (Loss) before cumulative effect of change in accounting principle per common share—diluted	$ (0.46)	$ 1.85	$ 1.84

EXHIBIT 2.1

THE DOW CHEMICAL COMPANY AND SUBSIDIARIES

For the years ended December 31	2001	2000	1999
Earnings (Loss) per common share—diluted	$ (0.43)	$ 1.85	$ 1.82
Common stock dividends declared per share of Dow common stock	$ 1.295	$ 1.16	$ 1.16
Weighted-average common shares outstanding—basic	901.8	893.2	874.9
Weighted-average common shares outstanding—diluted	901.8	904.5	893.5

Source: 10K for Dow Chemical Company, December 31, 2001.

EXHIBIT 2.2

The Dow Chemical Company and Subsidiaries

Consolidated Balance Sheets

At December 31	2001	2000
	(in millions)	
Assets		
Current Assets		
Cash and cash equivalents	$ 220	$ 278
Marketable securities and interest-bearing deposits	44	163
Accounts and notes receivable:		
Trade (net of allowance for doubtful receivables—2001: $123; 2000: $103)	2,868	3,655
Other	2,230	2,764

EXHIBIT 2.2

THE DOW CHEMICAL COMPANY AND SUBSIDIARIES

At December 31	2001	2000
		(in millions)
Inventories:		
Finished and work in process	3,569	3,396
Materials and supplies	871	817
Deferred income tax assets—current	506	250
Total current assets	10,308	11,323
Investments		
Investment in nonconsolidated affiliates	1,581	2,096
Other investments	1,663	2,528
Noncurrent receivables	802	674
Total investments	4,046	5,298
Property		
Property	35,890	34,852
Less accumulated depreciation	22,311	21,141
Net property	13,579	13,711
Other Assets		
Goodwill (net of accumulated amortization—2001: $569; 2000: $459)	3,130	1,928
Deferred income tax assets—noncurrent	2,248	1,968
Deferred charges and other assets	2,204	1,763
Total other assets	7,582	5,659
Total Assets	$ 35,515	$ 35,991
Liabilities and Stockholders' Equity		
Current Liabilities		
Notes payable	$ 1,209	$ 2,519
Long-term debt due within one year	408	318
Accounts payable:		
Trade	2,713	2,975

EXHIBIT 2.2

THE DOW CHEMICAL COMPANY AND SUBSIDIARIES

At December 31	2001	2000
		(in millions)
Other	926	1,594
Income taxes payable	190	258
Deferred income tax liabilities—current	236	35
Dividends payable	323	217
Accrued and other current liabilities	2,120	2,257
Total current liabilities	8,125	10,173
Long-Term Debt	9,266	6,613
Other Noncurrent Liabilities		
Deferred income tax liabilities—noncurrent	760	1,165
Pension and other postretirement benefits—noncurrent	2,475	2,238
Other noncurrent obligations	3,539	3,012
Total other noncurrent liabilities	6,774	6,415
Minority Interest in Subsidiaries	357	450
Preferred Securities of Subsidiaries	1,000	500
Stockholders' Equity		
Common stock (authorized 1,500,000,000 shares of $2.50 par value each; issued 981,377,562)	2,453	2,453
Additional paid-in capital	–	–
Unearned ESOP shares	(90)	(103)
Retained earnings	11,112	12,675
Accumulated other comprehensive loss	(1,070)	(560)
Treasury stock at cost (shares 2001: 76,540,276; 2000: 84,280,041)	(2,412)	(2,625)
Net stockholders' equity	9,993	11,840
Total Liabilities and Stockholders' Equity	$ 35,515	$ 35,991

Source: 10K for Dow Chemical Company, December 31, 2001

EXHIBIT 2.3

The Dow Chemical Company and Subsidiaries

Consolidated Statements of Comprehensive Income

For the years ended December 31	2001	2000	1999
			(in millions)
Net Income (Loss) Available for Common Stockholders	$ (385)	$ 1,675	$ 1,617
Other Comprehensive Income (Loss), Net of Tax (tax amounts shown below for 2001, 2000, 1999)			
Unrealized gains (losses) on investments:			
Unrealized holding gains (losses) during the period (less tax of $ (34), $20, $127)	(60)	35	213
Less: Reclassification adjustments for net amounts included in net income (loss) (less tax of $(152), $(4), $(31))	(259)	(8)	(52)
Cumulative translation adjustments (less tax of $(21), $(33), $(47))	(148)	(188)	(121)
Minimum pension liability adjustments (less tax of $(8), $5, $0)	(21)	12	–
Net loss on cash flow hedging derivative instruments (less tax of $(13) for 2001)	(22)	–	–
Total other comprehensive income (loss)	(510)	(149)	40
Comprehensive Income (Loss)	$ (895)	$ 1,526	$ 1,657

Source: 10K for Dow Chemical Company, December 31, 2001.

Revenue Recognition

In general, revenue is recognized (i.e., recorded) at the point of sale. When a customer makes a purchase, the transaction is completed, and the seller has a right to collect payment, the revenue can be recorded. Under the matching principle (matching the expenses incurred to accomplish a sale, with the revenues earned from the sale), the appropriate costs from the sale, such as cost of goods sold and sales commissions, are also recorded, and the profit is determined.

There are several broad issues that companies have to address when determining how to follow the general guidance. There are also some very specific ways to recognize revenue because of generally accepted accounting methods traditionally used in particular industries.

The broad issues, which require additional revenue recognition guidance, include sales with installment payments, contract sales, and sales with a right of return.

Installment sales are not the same as sales with installment collections of cash. The former would be accounted for using accrual accounting, which would apply the revenue recognition criteria in Exhibit 2.4. The latter involves sales that are collected over a number of years, like real estate sales, and may involve the risk of not collecting all payments. Such sales, with extended payment periods, may be accounted for using the installment sales method, which involves recording revenues in a specific proportion to the pattern of cash collections. For these sales in which uncollectibility risks are present, recognizing the revenue at the point of sale would overstate income. However, in order to use the installment sales method, certain criteria have to be met (like the lack of reasonable assurance as to the collection of the sale price). Companies have to make judgments as to the likelihood of collection of the sale price.

Contract sales may involve long-term construction-type contracts or long-term service contracts. As the obligation under the terms of the

EXHIBIT 2.4

Comparison of General Revenue Recognition Principles of U.S. GAAP and International Standards

U.S. GAAP*	IAS**
Revenues have been earned due to substantial completion of the earnings process.	The buyer has obtained the significant risks and rewards of ownership. The transaction's revenues and costs can be measured.
Revenues have been realized or are realizable.	The seller will probably obtain the economic benefits of the sale.

*U.S. Generally Accepted Accounting Principles.

**International Accounting Standards.

contract is fulfilled, the seller should recognize revenue (known as the percentage-of-completion method). When a business has done 50 percent of the work under contract, it should record 50 percent of the contracted price as revenue. Of course, using this method depends on good estimates of costs and progress and getting the work done. Often, the amount of cost incurred relative to the total cost budgeted is used as a surrogate for the percentage of work completed.

Sales with a right of return present the problem of when to recognize revenue because a sale reversed, in theory, is a sale that should not be recorded as revenue. According to generally accepted accounting principles (GAAP), revenue in these circumstances should be recognized at the time of the sale if all of the following conditions are met:

- The seller's price to the buyer is substantially fixed or determinable at the date of sale.
- The buyer has paid the seller, or the buyer is obligated to pay the seller and the obligation is not contingent on resale of the product.
- The buyer's obligation to the seller would not be changed in the event of theft or physical destruction or damage of the product.
- The buyer acquiring the product for resale has economic substance apart from that provided by the seller.
- The seller does not have significant obligations for future performance to directly bring about resale of the product by the buyer.
- The amount of future returns can be reasonably estimated.[2]

With all the possibilities and all the industry practices, it is important to find out what a particular company's revenue recognition policy is. Most companies describe their revenue recognition policies, in varying degrees of clarity, whether in the notes to the financial statements, or the management discussion and analysis (MD&A) or in both places. Exhibit 2.5 shows an example of disclosure in Dow Chemical's annual report.

EXHIBIT 2.5

Dow Chemical 2001 Annual Report

Note A: Revenue

Sales are recognized when the revenue is realized or realizable, and has been earned. In general, revenue is recognized as risk and title to the product transfers to the customer, which usually occurs at the time shipment is made; as services are rendered; or in relation to licensee production levels.

IN THE REAL WORLD

Round-Trip Revenue

It is important to examine a company's revenue recognition policies. Sometimes, it may appear that companies are being overly optimistic when recognizing revenue; for example, if all the money received for a three-year contract is reported as being earned in the first year. Another questionable situation is referred to as *round-trip revenue*, wherein it appears that two companies simply exchange cash or asset amounts in some type of transaction and then report a revenue. For example, Elan Corporation, a drug company based in Ireland, engages in transactions with numerous research and development joint ventures. According to *The Wall Street Journal*, Elan "invests $20 million in a partner and the joint venture, and the venture immediately pays Elan $15 million for a medical technology license. Elan books that as revenue." The problem is that the $20 million is reported as an investment (an asset), so there is no apparent expense that results from "earning" the $15 million. "In effect, Elan converts $15 million of money it already had into new revenue." A financial statement reader should always make an effort to thoroughly understand how a company earns and records (or recognizes) its revenues.

Source: Jesse Eisinger, "Research Partnerships Give Irish Drug Maker Rosy Financial Glow," *The Wall Street Journal*, January 30, 2002, A1.

Types of Earnings

Starting at the top of the example income statement as shown in Exhibit 2.6, one typically sees a sales revenue or net sales revenue. Since GAAP require this to be an accrual-basis revenue rather than a cash-basis revenue, it is an amount that reflects what a company has earned, not just what cash it has received. The sales revenue could represent a combination of cash sales, the earning of cash the company received in a previ-

EXHIBIT 2.6

Multistep Income Statement

XYZ Company
Income Statement
For the year ended December 31, XXXX

Net sales		$20,000
Less:	Cost of sales	(100)
Gross profit		19,900
Less:	Depreciation expense	(100)
	Selling, general, and administrative expenses	(100)
Earnings from operations		19,700
Less or Plus:	Minority interest	(100)
	Goodwill amortization	(100)
	Restructuring charges	(100)
	Equity in affiliate earnings	100
Earnings before interest expense and income taxes		19,500
Less:	Interest expense	(100)
Earnings before income taxes		19,400
Less:	Income taxes	(100)
Net earnings from continuing operations		19,300
Discontinued operations, charges (net of taxes)		(100)
Extraordinary items (net of taxes)		(100)
Cumulative effect of change in accounting principle (net of taxes)		(100)
Net earnings		$19,000

EXHIBIT 2.6

Single-Step Income Statement

XYZ Company
Income Statement
For the year ended December 31, XXXX

Net sales	$20,000
Less: Cost of sales	(100)
Depreciation expense	(100)
Selling, general, and administrative expenses	(100)
Minority interest	(100)
Goodwill amortization	(100)
Restructuring charges	(100)
Equity in affiliate earnings	100
Earnings before interest expense and income taxes	19,500
Less: Interest expense	(100)
Income taxes	(100)
Net earnings from continuing operations	19,300
Discontinued operations, charges (net of taxes)	(100)
Extraordinary items (net of taxes)	(100)
Cumulative effect of change in accounting principle (net of taxes)	(100)
Net earnings	$19,000

ous period, and the earning of cash the company may receive in a future period. In general, the sales revenue represents what a company has earned performing its normal operations. The recognition of revenue can actually be quite complicated and controversial. The SEC is investigating many companies for their revenue recognition practices.

From top to bottom, the income statement reflects a process of including the more expected results to the less expected results, the costs more directly related to operations to the costs less directly related. Therefore, somewhat toward the end of the income statement, there may be included those items that earnings press releases may remove from their net income in order to report more regular net income, say, without restructuring charges. Exhibit 2.6 shows an example of a multistep income statement, and includes some of the line items and subtotals that a company might report.

TIPS & TECHNIQUES

SEC Staff Accounting Bulletin: No. 101—Revenue Recognition in Financial Statements

The Securities and Exchange Commission (SEC) published Staff Accounting Bulletin (SAB) No. 101 (December 3, 1999) because of a number of circumstances, including a Treadway Commission report that indicated that the majority of financial reporting frauds in their ten-year study (1987–1997) involved overstating revenue.

SAB No. 101 sets forth the revenue recognition criteria as:

> The staff believes that revenue generally is realized or realizable and earned when all of the following criteria are met:

- Persuasive evidence of an arrangement exists
- Delivery has occurred or services have been rendered
- The seller's price to the buyer is fixed or determinable, and
- Collectibility is reasonably assured.

For many hypothetical scenarios, questions, and interpretive responses, go to *http://www.sec.gov/interps/account/sab101.htm.*

The organization and order of the information in this example are typical. But some companies do not include the subtotals gross profit and earnings from operations; they may just subtract all the expenses before the interest and income taxes and call that subtotal earnings before interest and taxes (EBIT). An example of a single-step income statement is also shown in Exhibit 2.6.

Operating Income

As strange as this may sound, *operating income* is *not* the same thing as *income from continuing operations*. The latter is further down on the income statement, in fact, because it is the result of subtracting interest expense and income taxes from operating income. The income statements of both Duke Energy and Southern Company (see Exhibits 3.3 and 3.4 in Chapter 3) are good, clear examples that show the distinction between operating income and income from continuing operations. Notice that in both cases, operating revenues minus operating expenses results in operating income. Sometimes, operating income is referred to as EBIT, earnings before interest and taxes. Note that for both Duke and Southern, the main

TIPS & TECHNIQUES

There are several different titles that may be used for the income statement, any one of which a particular company might choose. They all contain the same basic information. The income statement can be identified by the fact that sales revenue is at the top and earnings per share is close to the bottom. Examples of those titles are:

- Consolidated Statements of Operations
- Consolidated Statements of Earnings
- Consolidated Statements of Income

two line items subtracted from operating income are interest expense and income taxes, to arrive at income from continuing operations. If one needs information about EBITDA, another common measure, it is a matter of adding depreciation and amortization (both of which are shown in our examples under operating expense) to operating income. Some companies do not show depreciation and amortization explicitly in the income statement, but the information can be found in the operating section of the cash flow statement or in the notes. In Exhibit 2.6, the hypothetical example shows earnings from operations (which could be identified as XYZ's operating income). But the "earnings before interest expense and income taxes" could also be identified as XYZ's operating

IN THE REAL WORLD

EBITDA

EBITDA is earnings before interest, taxes, depreciation, and amortization. Users of EBITDA may say that it is a better indication than GAAP net income of a company's operating results. However, Alfred M. King has a dire warning that EBITDA is "one of the most flawed concepts to be adopted by the financial community." To refute the idea that EBITDA is closer to an operating cash flow than is net income, he points out that interest payments and tax payments are cash outflows that take priority and are unavoidable, so ignoring them is not realistic. King implies that since GAAP financial statements already provide better cash flow and earnings information in the statement of cash flows and the income statement, the reporting of EBITDA by companies may be motivated by the desire to make a situation look better than it really is or, in the case of start-up companies, even to avoid having to focus on their operating at a loss.

Source: Alfred M. King, "Warning: Use of EBITDA May Be Dangerous to Your Career," *Strategic Finance*, September 2001, 35–37.

income. Dow's annual report actually refers to the "Earnings before Interest, Income Taxes, and Minority Interests" of $35 million (see the income statement in Exhibit 2.1) as EBIT in its MD&A. The lack of strict standardization in the definition of operating income makes it necessary to be careful to be consistent when comparing companies and to be aware of how investment research firms are calculating their numbers when analyzing companies' and industries' financial data and ratios.

Discontinued Operations

The three line items below earnings from continuing operations are not considered regularly recurring items, so they are separated out and reported net of their tax effect. Discontinued operations relate to sale or abandonment of a major segment or subsidiary of a company. This line item could include two components: the net income or loss from operating the discontinued operating during the year (or part of the year), and the gain or loss on the actual disposal.

Extraordinary Items

Extraordinary items have two characteristics. They are unusual in nature, and they are infrequent in occurrence. These criteria were designed to be fairly difficult to meet, but there is one circumstance that the FASB decided would be extraordinary by definition, without meeting the criteria. Gains and losses on early extinguishments of debt are reported as extraordinary so that companies will not manipulate their income from continuing operations by strategic timing of paying off debt.

Cumulative Effect of Change in Accounting Principle

If a company changes from one accounting principle to another, whether by choice or by requirement from a new FASB statement or

SEC Staff Accounting Bulletin, the cumulative effect of that change may be required to be reported on the income statement. Dow's income statement shows a cumulative effect of $32 million, and it is explained in both the notes, as follows:

> *Accounting for Derivative Instruments and Hedging Activities*
>
> Effective January 1, 2001, the Company adopted SFAS No. 133, as amended by SFAS No. 137 and SFAS No. 138, and as interpreted by the FASB and the Derivatives Implementation Group through "Statement 133 Implementation Issues." The adoption of SFAS No. 133 resulted in the Company recording a transition adjustment gain of $32 (net of related income tax of $19) in net income and a net transition adjustment gain of $65 (net of related income tax of $38) in AOCI at January 1, 2001. (Dow Chemical, Notes to the Consolidated Financial Statements, p. 55)

and in the auditors' report, as follows:

> As discussed in Notes A and J to the consolidated financial statements, effective January 1, 2001, The Dow Chemical Company changed its method of accounting for derivative instruments and hedging activities to conform to Statement of Financial Accounting Standards No. 133. (Dow Chemical, Independent Auditors' Report, p. 40)

Comprehensive Income

The definition of *comprehensive income* is

> the change in equity of a business enterprise during a period from transactions and other events and circumstances from nonowner sources. It includes all changes in equity during a period except those resulting form investments by owners and distribution to owners. (Statement of Financial Accounting Concepts No. 6)

Equity means property rights and refers to stockholders' or owners' equity. This owners' equity represents the claims of owners to the assets of the business, as shown in the accounting equation:

$$\text{Assets} = \text{Liabilities} + \text{Equity}$$

When the company reports net income on its income statement, that income amount is added to the stockholders' equity or property rights. Therefore, the components of net income affect equity. Those components of net income are limited to revenues, expenses, gains, and losses. All of those components of net income are included in comprehensive income. But there are changes in stockholders' equity that are comprehensive income but not net income. Some changes in assets and liabilities go right to the stockholders' equity section of the balance sheet without first affecting net income and being included in the income statement. Unrealized gains and losses that are included in comprehensive income but are not recognized or reported on the income statement are related to foreign currency translation adjustments, available-for-sale investments, and derivative financial instruments.

Requirement

The FASB requires companies to report comprehensive income, either in a separate financial statement (as Dow Chemical Company does, shown in Exhibit 2.3) or as part of the stockholders' equity statement. The definition of comprehensive income given earlier relates it to the change in equity during a period, but it is also described as the change in wealth during a period. Wealth can increase not only from business operations but also from changes in market values that are not related to operations. The goal of the requirement to report comprehensive income is to have a net income with results of business operations and a separate comprehensive income with results of the market's impact on the values of assets and liabilities. Three examples of items affecting comprehensive income are (1) foreign currency translation adjustments, (2) unrealized gains and losses on available-for-sale securities, and (3) deferred gains and losses on derivative financial instruments.

Foreign Currency Translation Adjustments

When changes in the value of foreign currency cause the assets of a company to increase in value, the result will be an increase in the stockholders' equity (picture the accounting equation increasing on the left side as well as on the right side). Because the change in value of the foreign currency is not related to the company's operations, the increase in stockholders' equity cannot be reported as net income. However, the increase in stockholders' equity is reported as comprehensive income.

Unrealized Gains and Losses on Available-for-Sale Securities

Companies that own investments in marketable securities (bonds and stocks) will see the market values of their investments increase and/or decrease over time. If that investment is classified as "available for sale" (meaning that the company does not intend to sell but could if necessary, as contrasted with "trading" investments not intended to be held a long time), then the investment must be included in the balance sheet at its market value. If that market value is greater than the cost of the investment, there is an unrealized holding gain. But the gain in value is not related to the company's operations and the company is in the same situation as for the foreign currency change discussed above: an increase in asset value that must be balanced with an increase in stockholders' equity that cannot be reported as net income. Therefore, it is comprehensive income.

Deferred Gains and Losses on Derivative Financial Instruments

Companies may invest in derivative financial instruments to hedge their exposure to the risk of changing prices or rates. Such changes will cause the value of the derivative to change, and again, lead to unrealized gains or losses. If the derivative instrument meets certain criteria, the unrealized gain or loss will be reported in comprehensive income rather than in net income.

The Analysis of Profitability

The financial analysis of an organization is of interest to parties that intend to make decisions about associating with that organization in some way, whether to invest in it, work for it, recommend it, or any other possibility. In general, one wants to be associated with successful (rather than otherwise) organizations. For a company, success has many dimensions. Practically everything a for-profit company does can be seen as a financing activity, an investing activity, or an operating activity. A company that is successful in these three areas will be successful overall. We can measure overall success in the three areas, financing, investing, and operating, by looking at the components of return on equity (ROE). ROE is one of several "return on ___" ratios that have some measure of income in the numerator and a financial statement component in the denominator.

The basic calculation of ROE is:

$$\text{ROE} = \text{Net income/Stockholders' equity}$$

ROE can be broken down to reflect return on assets (ROA) and financial leverage (FL) as follows:

$$\begin{aligned}\text{ROE} &= \text{Net income/Stockholders' equity}\\ &= (\text{Net income/Total assets}) \times (\text{Total assets/Stockholders' equity})\\ &= \text{ROA} \times \text{FL}\end{aligned}$$

ROA can be further broken down into profit margin (PM, also called return on sales) and asset turnover (ATO):

$$\begin{aligned}\text{ROE} &= (\text{Net income/Total assets}) \times \text{FL}\\ &= (\text{Net income/Sales}) \times (\text{Sales/Total assets}) \times \text{FL}\\ &= \text{Profit margin} \times \text{Asset turnover} \times \text{FL}\\ &= \text{PM} \times \text{ATO} \times \text{FL}\end{aligned}$$

We end up with a measure of success (ROE) made up of three components:

1. Profit margin (PM)—to reflect the operating success of a company
2. Asset turnover (ATO)—to reflect the investing success of a company
3. Financial leverage (FL)—to reflect the financing activities of a company

These are broad generalizations, and there are variations within each category. The margin ratios generally compare one line item of the income statement to another. The turnover ratios (also called asset management ratios[3]) compare information on the income statement to information on the balance sheet. The financial leverage and other liquidity and solvency ratios compare parts of the balance sheet to other parts of the balance sheet. Exhibit 2.7 illustrates an overview of these ratios and how they relate to the financial statements:

Profitability

Of the five separately identifiable ratios in the ROE model above (ROE, ROA, PM, ATO, and FL), three are related to profitability because they relate net income (net profit) to another financial statement amount.

EXHIBIT 2.7

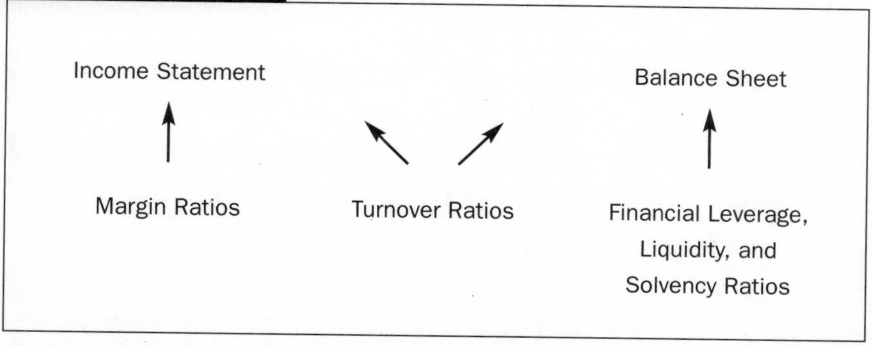

ROE indicates how successfully the company is using the owners' (shareholders') investment to produce profits. ROA indicates how well the company is using assets to produce profits. Return on sales (or profit margin) indicates how much of its sales revenue a company is able to keep as profit.

For Dow Chemical Company (in Exhibit 2.8), the ROE shows that the company in 2000 was earning a profit of about 14.2 cents per dollar of investment by stockholders, but it went to a loss of about 4 cents per dollar in 2001 (a 127 percent drop). Dow's ROA also declined, from 4.7 cents of profit per dollar of assets to a loss of 1 cent per dollar (a 123 percent drop). The return on sales (ROS) or profit margin went from about 5.7 cents of profit to 1.4 cents of loss per dollar of sales (a 124 percent drop).

Return on Assets

A more in-depth analysis of ROA is possible. According to Palepu, Bernard, and Healy (1997)[4], the traditional measure of ROA is internally inconsistent since the denominator is total assets and represents all the resources or capital provided by both creditors and owners. However, the numerator is net income (after deduction of interest expense) and therefore represents profits available only to stockholders. A more internally consistent (since both numerator and denominator include debt-related information) measure of profitability is

$$\text{Preinterest ROA} = \text{EBILAT/Assets} = \frac{\text{Net income} + \text{Interest expense} \times (1 - \text{tax rate})}{\text{Assets}}$$

EBILAT is earnings before interest, less adjusted taxes.

Adding back the after-tax interest yields a numerator that now represents profits available to creditors or interest-bearing debt and stockholders. A further modification is even better because it removes from the denominator, assets financed by non-interest-bearing debt (since the

EXHIBIT 2.8

Dow Chemical Company

Overall Performance

	2001	2000
		(amounts in millions)
ROE:	$(385)/$9,993 = –0.0385	$1,675/$11,840 = 0.1415
ROA:	$(385)/$35,515 = –0.0108	$1,675/$35,991 = 0.0465
ROS:	$(385)/$27,805 = –0.0138	$1,675/$29,534 = 0.0567

Modifications of ROA

	2001	2000

Preinterest ROA

$$\frac{\text{NI} + \text{Interest } (1 - \text{tax rate})}{\text{Assets}}$$

$$\frac{\$(385) + \$733(1 - .35)}{\$35{,}515} = 0.0026 \qquad \frac{\$1{,}675 + 665(1 - .35)}{\$35{,}991} = 0.0585$$

RONA (or ROC)

$$\frac{\text{NI} + \text{Interest } (1 - \text{tax rate})}{\text{Equity} + \text{Debt}}$$

$$\frac{\$(385) + \$733\ (1 - .35)}{\$9{,}993 + \$10{,}475} = 0.0045 \qquad \frac{\$1{,}675 + \$665\ (1 - .35)}{\$11{,}840 + 9{,}132} = 0.1005$$

Operating ROA

$$\frac{\text{NI} + (\text{Int exp} - \text{Int inc}) \times (1 - \text{tax rate})}{\text{Equity} + \text{Debt} - \text{Cash} + \text{Short-term investments}}$$

$$\frac{\$(385) + (\$733 - \$85)(1 - .35)}{\$9{,}993 + \$10{,}475 - \$264} = \frac{\$36.2}{\$20{,}204} = 0.0018$$

$$\frac{\$1{,}675 + (\$665 - \$146)(1 - .35)}{\$11{,}840 + \$9{,}132 - \$441} = \frac{\$2{,}012.35}{\$20{,}531} = 0.0980$$

numerator does not contain earnings available to non-interest-bearing debt).

$$\text{RONA (or ROC)} = \frac{\text{Net income + Interest expense} \times (1 - \text{tax rate})}{\text{Equity + Interest-bearing debt}}$$

Return on net assets (RONA) or return on capital (ROC) improves on the preinterest ROA by modifying the denominator to include only interest-bearing debt along with the equity. That way, the ratio compares earnings available to owners and creditors to the assets that can be claimed by those owners and creditors.

Another measure of ROA focuses on operations. Operating ROA is derived by removing cash and short-term investments from the denominator and simultaneously removing the earnings of the cash and short-term investments from the numerator.

$$\text{Operating ROA} = \frac{\text{Net income + (Interest expense} - \text{Interest income)} \times (1 - \text{tax rate})}{\text{Equity + Debt} - \text{Cash and short-term investments}}$$

Ideally, the criterion against which to evaluate the RONA would be the weighted average cost of debt and equity capital. According to Palepu, Bernard & Healy, "In the long run, the value of the firm is determined by where RONA (or ROC) stands relative to this norm."[5] The drawback is the complexity of calculating the cost of equity in order to derive the weighted average. Exhibit 2.8 includes the modifications of ROA for Dow Chemical for the years 2000 and 2001.

Profit Margin and Other Margins

The return on sales (ROS) is derived from the ROE model reviewed here:

$$\underset{\text{ROE}}{\frac{\text{Net income}}{\text{Stockholders' equity}}} = \underset{\text{ROA}}{\frac{\text{Net income}}{\text{Assets}}} \times \underset{\text{FL}}{\frac{\text{Assets}}{\text{St. Equity}}} = \underset{\text{ROS}}{\frac{\text{Net income}}{\text{Sales}}} \times \underset{\text{ATO}}{\frac{\text{Sales}}{\text{Assets}}} \times \underset{\text{FL}}{\frac{\text{Assets}}{\text{St. Equity}}}$$

$$\qquad\qquad\qquad\qquad\qquad\qquad\qquad\text{Operating} \qquad \text{Investing} \qquad \text{Financing}$$

The ROS is also known as the profit margin. Net income is the bottom line on the income statement, and of course sales revenue is the first

TIPS & TECHNIQUES

Operating ROA

Operating ROA can be calculated in a more straightforward and easily remembered way.

$$\text{Operating ROA} = \frac{\text{Operating income}}{\text{Operating assets}}$$

For operating income, use EBIT, and for operating assets, use current assets.

line item. So the PM is the last line as a percentage of the first line and therefore shows how much of every dollar of sales a company can report as profit. Improving a PM (increasing it) can result from cutting costs relative to sales.

Just as there are modifications of the ROA ratio, there are modifications to the PM. They all come from substituting various subtotals on the income statement for the net income in the numerator of the PM ratio. Some variations are (working down from the top of the income statement):

$$\text{Gross PM rate} = \frac{\text{Gross PM}}{\text{Sales}} = \frac{\text{Sales} - \text{Cost of sales}}{\text{Sales}}$$

$$\text{EBITDA margin rate} = \frac{\text{EBITDA}}{\text{Sales}}$$

$$\text{Operating PM rate} = \frac{\text{Operating income}}{\text{Sales}}$$

$$\text{OR} \quad \frac{\text{EBIT}}{\text{Sales}}$$

$$\text{Pretax margin rate} = \frac{\text{Income before income taxes}}{\text{Sales}}$$

As mentioned before, these margin ratios concern the success of the company's operations. All of these margin ratios will actually show up in what is referred to as common-sized income statements (covered in Chapter 6), prepared from multistep income statements that include subtotals. Exhibit 2.9 shows the margin ratios for Dow Chemical. The margin ratios do not become negative in 2001 until after interest is deducted.

Earnings per Share

EPS is the traditional measure of the relationship between a company's profits and the ownership interest of the company's common shareholders. It is the most widely used financial ratio. GAAP require that

IN THE REAL WORLD

GAAP EPS versus PRO FORMA EPS

Financial statement users and analysts find information from many different sources. However, they should be aware that this information may differ in its credibility, as illustrated by some companies' press releases. For example, First Data, a payment services provider in Greenwood Village, Colorado, reported its third-quarter earnings with a headline that announced a 19 percent growth in earnings per share (EPS). However, the important thing to remember is that the FASB, which determines GAAP for financial statements, does not have authority over news releases. So, the result may be that GAAP EPS may differ from the EPS reported in the newspaper (sometimes referred to as pro forma EPS). GAAP EPS must include all of a company's expenses and losses. Pro forma EPS are frequently calculated as if certain expenses or losses did not exist. That enables a company to paint a rosier picture of its operating results in the newspaper. It's very important to be aware of what the numbers are and how they were obtained.

See Jonathan Weil, "Ignore the Items Behind the Curtain: EPS Means Different Things to Different Earnings," *WSJ*, October 16, 2001.

EXHIBIT 2.9

Dow Chemical Company Margin Ratios

		2001		2000	
Gross profit margin	=				
Gross profit / Sales	=	$27,805 – 23,652 / $27,805	= 0.1494	$29,534 – 24,131 / $29,534	= 0.1829
EBITDA margin	=				
EBITDA / Sales	=	$35 + 1,815 / $27,805	= 0.0665	$3,105 + 1,738 / $29,534	= 0.1640
Operating profit margin	=				
Operating income / Sales	=	$35 / $27,805	= 0.0013	$3,105 / $29,534	= 0.1051
Pretax margin	=				
Income before income taxes / Sales	=	$(613) / $27,805	= –0.0220	$2,586 / $29,534	= 0.0876
Profit margin	=				
Net income / Sales	=	$(385) / $27,805	= –0.0138	$1,675 / $29,534	= 0.0567

EPS be reported on the income statement after net income. EPS reports the amount of net income available to common shareholders for each share of common stock outstanding. Therefore, the actual net income may be adjusted for amounts that are not related to common shareholders (e.g., dividends on preferred stock would be deducted from net income to get income available to common shareholders). The denominator is the weighted average of common shares outstanding only. Notice that Dow reports basic EPS and diluted EPS both before and after the cumulative effect of the change in accounting principle. Basic EPS is computed as follow:

$$\text{Basic EPS} = \frac{\text{Net income available to common shareholders}}{\text{Weighted average number of common shares outstanding}}$$

Diluted EPS, if reported, is equal to or lower than basic EPS because its purpose is to demonstrate how much of a reduction might occur in the EPS if securities such as stock options or convertible preferred stock, that will result in additional outstanding common shares, are converted. Dow apparently does not have any potentially dilutive securities, so basic EPS is equal to diluted EPS.

Price/Earnings Ratio

One of the uses of the EPS of a company is to calculate the price/earnings (P/E) ratio as follows:

$$\text{P/E ratio} = \frac{\text{Market value per share}}{\text{Earnings per share}}$$

The market value per share is the stock price on any given day, so the P/E ratio can change frequently. The P/E ratio indicates how much value the market places on the company relative to its earnings. The conventional wisdom is that a low P/E ratio may indicate an undervalued stock, whereas a high P/E ratio may indicate an overvalued stock. Or a high P/E ratio may indicate that the market has high expectations for the company (i.e., that it will grow in the future). Exhibit 2.10 shows Dow's

EXHIBIT 2.10

Comparing Dow Chemical's P/E Ratio

	Company	Industry	Sector	S&P 500
P/E ratio	92.54	43.51	34.31	29.95

P/E ratio at May 19, 2002, compared to the industry, the sector, and the Standard & Poor's 500 (obtained from Multex.com). It appears that the market is very optimistic about Dow's future.

The P/E ratio is one of several price multiples, all of which compare the stock price to some other financial information. Exhibits 2.11 and 2.12 show the Fortune 500's top ten ROAs and ROEs and the

IN THE REAL WORLD

Financial Analysis: Looking at the Big Picture: Red Flags

The purpose of financial analysis, for many who are involved in it, is to make investment decisions. According to Alfred Rappaport, the wary investor should look for signals that a company's stock price may be "headed for a fall." He explains a number of those signals, some of which involve more in-depth means of information gathering. Rappaport's seven red flags are:

1. *Ambiguous business models.* Judging a business model involves examining whether it makes economic sense. This is difficult for companies that are new, like Internet businesses, or companies that change, like Enron did from selling natural gas to trading energy.

In the Real World continued

2. *Opaque financial reports.* Reported earnings may not be what it appears to be since companies can use discretion about what to include and when to include it. One indication may be whether reported earnings are consistently greater than operating cash flows. Another indication may be a rate of return below the cost of capital.

3. *Earnings expectations games.* Investors should be aware that beating earnings expectations may not mean that the company is performing incredibly well but that the company skillfully managed expectations down.

4. *Price wars.* In highly competitive, commodity-type businesses in which selling price is almost the only way to differentiate products, a price war may erupt. Some companies benefit; some suffer, typically those that are not industry leaders.

5. *Value-destroying mergers and acquisitions.* History shows that typically stock value does not benefit from mergers and acquisitions.

6. *Uneconomic share buybacks.* Investors should find out why the buyback is occurring, and be wary if it seems to be for no business reason other than to affect EPS dilution.

7. *Shareholder-unfriendly executive compensation practices.* These types of compensation plans seem to arise from the fact that stock option values have declined. The plans appear to be structured to reward executives' regard of their ability to make the company successful. Beware if executive's interests are not aligned with corporate interests.

The red flags above involve looking beyond the financial statements, into the footnotes, and even beyond those into any information made public by a company that may affect the situations discussed above.

Source: Alfred Rappaport, "To Avoid a Tumble, Look for These Red Flags," *The Wall Street Journal*, February 25, 2002, B5.

EXHIBIT 2.11

Fortune 500 Industries with the Top Ten ROAs and ROEs in 2001

Return on Assets	%	Return on Shareholders' Equity	%
1. Pharmaceuticals	16.3	1. Pharmaceuticals	33.2
2. Household and personal products	9.5	2. Household and personal products	26.4
3. Beverages	8.1	3. Beverages	25.2
4. Apparel	7.0	4. Food consumer products	20.8
5. Food consumer products	6.4	5. Homebuilders	19.6
6. Publishing, printing	6.3	6. Diversified financials	19.3
7. Homebuilders	5.8	7. Petroleum refining	18.6
8. Wholesalers, diversified	5.8	8. Mining, crude-oil production	15.6
9. Petroleum refining	5.7	9. Chemicals	15.0
10. Chemicals	5.6	10. Apparel	14.6

Source: *Fortune* magazine, April 15, 2002, F-1–F-20.

EXHIBIT 2.12

Fortune 500 Companies with the Top Ten ROAs and ROEs in 2001

Return on Assets	%	Return on Shareholders' Equity	%
1. Kindred Healthcare	34.7	1. General Mills	1274.1
2. Oracle	23.2	2. Tricon Global Restaurants	473.1
3. Sara Lee	22.3	3. Maytag	202.7
4. Oxford Health Plans	20.4	4. Sara Lee	202.0
5. Caremark Rx	20.3	5. Colgate-Palmolive	135.5
6. Pfizer	19.9	6. Kindred Healthcare	88.6
7. Bristol-Myers Squibb	19.4	7. Aramark	71.5
8. CDW Computer Centers	18.0	8. Oxford Health Plans	69.6
9. Coca-Cola	17.7	9. Wyeth	56.1
10. Amgen	17.4	10. Pitney Bowes	54.8

Source: *Fortune* magazine, April 15, 2002, F-1–F-20.

IN THE REAL WORLD

The Goodwill Write-Off

What is this thing called the Goodwill Write-off? It's a kind of new thing because accounting standards have changed. Goodwill is an intangible asset created when a company buys another company and pays more than the market value of its net assets. That excess of purchase price over market value of net assets recognizes that the company has some inherent intangible value not reflected in the recorded assets and liabilities. Companies previously amortized that intangible asset over some assumed life, resulting in a noncash expense on the income statement. Now goodwill is to be carried on the books as an asset until it is permanently impaired. When impaired, the entire amount of goodwill, or some big portion of it, is written off. Write-offs by big companies are announced in press releases such as the following:

> Qwest Communications International, Inc., expects to take a charge of $20 billion to $30 billion this year to reflect a decline in the value of assets it has acquired. . . .

The goodwill charge reduces net income by a large amount but does not affect cash from operations. As a result, the market does not tend to see it as enormously bad news.

Source: "Qwest Expects to Take a Charge Related to Goodwill of $20 Billion to $30 Billion," *The Wall Street Journal*, April 2, 2002.

corresponding companies. The other price multiples are discussed in Chapter 6.

Summary

A company has to be profitable in the long run to be successful. Traditionally, the focus has been on the income statement as the main source of information about profitability. Since the income statement is prepared on the accrual basis, a lot of judgment goes into deciding when certain economic activity meets the right criteria to be reported in the income statement. Revenue recognition especially has been under a lot of scrutiny lately. In addition, there is so much motivation for companies to downplay some expenses as not regular enough for decision makers to pay any attention to. These aspects of financial reporting present a challenge to those trying to evaluate a company's profitability. However, there are quite a few analytical techniques, like ROI, ROE, EPS, and the P/E ratio, that enable decision makers to assess the profitability of companies.

CHAPTER 3

Analyzing Liquidity and Solvency

After reading this chapter, you will be able to

- Understand how financial statements convey information about liquidity
- Evaluate the liquidity of a business
- Calculate ratios used to evaluate liquidity
- Understand the concept of solvency
- Understand how financial leverage affects a company and can be measured
- Understand the auditor's role in assessing going concern status
- Evaluate the solvency of a business
- Apply Altman's Z analysis to a business

Analyzing Liquidity

Analyzing the liquidity of a company involves examining the relationship between current assets and current liabilities to determine whether the company can fulfill its obligations for current liabilities in the short run. Solvency relates to a long-run perspective of the company's ability to pay its debts and whether it is a going concern.

Many of the companies that declare bankruptcy get to the point where they do not have adequate cash flow and are pushed over the edge by the calling of a loan or the loss of a line of credit. At this point, lending institutions no longer think that the company is a good risk. A thorough financial analysis includes looking at a company's financial statements through the eyes of a banker. Bankers want to know whether companies can make interest and principal payments on loans. Because of this need, a company's cash flow and working capital management are important. How can these areas be assessed?

Assessing Working Capital and Its Components

The term *working capital* truly means "current assets," but in common use is used to signify net working capital. Net working capital (which will be referred to as simply working capital) is the difference between current assets and current liabilities. Current assets are those that are expected to be liquidated or converted to cash within a year. Current liabilities are expected to be settled within a year. These are the broad descriptions of current assets and liabilities. Analysts are actually interested primarily in certain current assets and certain current liabilities, ones that may subsequently involve a cash flow. For example, accounts receivable results in a cash inflow to the company. Prepaid insurance does not refer to a subsequent cash flow, but rather to a period of time covered by insurance. Accounts payable results in a cash outflow for the company, and unearned revenue is a liability to fulfill that will result in a company's earning some cash already received.

So, overall, an analysis of working capital management will (should) focus on receivables and payables rather than prepaid items and unearned revenue. In addition, this analysis typically also involves inventory because its sale will result in a cash inflow.

New working capital = Current assets − Current liabilities

OR = Cash + Accounts rec. + Inventory − Accounts payable

Working capital ratio = Current assets ÷ Current liabilities

OR = (Cash + Accounts rec. + Inventory) ÷ Accounts payable

EXHIBIT 3.1

Current Ratio on May 22, 2002

	Company	**Industry**	**Sector**	**S&P 500**
Southern Company	0.71	0.83	0.85	1.69
Duke Energy	0.90	0.83	0.85	1.69
Wal-Mart	1.01	1.36	1.38	1.69
Kmart	1.75	1.36	1.38	1.69

Southern and Duke are in the utilities sector and electric utilities industry. Wal-Mart and Kmart are in the services sector and retail (department and discount) industry.

Source: Multex.com.

The working capital ratio is also called the current ratio. The current ratio should be high enough but not too high: high enough to show that current liabilities will be met but not so high that it signifies idle cash or too many resources tied up in current assets like inventory. A current ratio tells one how much in current assets is available to cover each dollar of liabilities. It is important to have the right mix of current assets and current liabilities for the type of company and the industry. Exhibit 3.1 shows the current ratio for four companies, for their industries and sectors, and for the Standard & Poor's 500.

The main components of working capital are examined to find out how productively the company is using its current assets and liabilities (turnover ratios) and how efficient the company is (represented by number of days related to a turnover).

Several turnover ratios involving current accounts are:

Current asset turnover = Sales/Current assets
Working capital turnover = Sales/Current assets – Current liabilities
Accounts receivable turnover = Sales/Accounts receivable
Inventory turnover = Cost of goods sold/Inventory
Accounts payable turnover = Purchases/Accounts payable
OR = Cost of goods sold/Accounts payable

Each turnover ratio represents a comparison of information on the income statement (e.g., sales) to information on the balance sheet (e.g., current assets). In general, for the asset turnover, one might say "the higher the better," and for the liability turnover "the lower the better." The results are sometimes expressed as a "number of times," but another practical interpretation involves examining how many dollars of sales are generated for each dollar of an asset. For example, if Company A has sales of $2 million and current assets of $1 million, then its current assets turnover is equal to $2 million ÷ $1 million or two times; the company generated $2.00 in sales for every $1.00 in current assets controlled by the company. These turnover ratios are discussed and illustrated as activity measures in Chapter 4.

Bankers are interested in management's ability to manage working capital and may establish minimum current ratio requirements in loan agreements. A violation of the loan covenant restriction may lead to the bank's considering the loan to be in default, which may lead to the bank's requiring immediate payment of the loan. If the company cannot make such payment, it may be necessary to file for bankruptcy. The world's greatest business plan and prospects for long-run solvency may be undermined by a current asset crunch. The next section describes a few more ways to measure liquidity.

Other Liquidity Ratios

The quick ratio, or acid-test ratio, is a stricter measure of liquidity than the current ratio. It is based on total quick assets rather than total current assets.

Quick ratio = Total quick assets/Total current liabilities

Quick assets include cash, investment securities, and net receivables, all only one step from being converted to cash. Inventory, in contrast, is two steps from cash: (1) inventory must be sold, and (2) the account receivable must be collected. Prepaid items never become cash. A company needs to maintain a quick ratio that is neither too low nor too high. A ratio that is too high indicates inefficient use of resources. For example, excess cash could be invested, excess inventory could be reduced (perhaps with just-in-time processes), and excess accounts receivable might indicate a collection problem. A ratio that is too low is a sign of possible cash shortages. The important thing is to know what is appropriate for the industry. Many investment research companies and websites provide industry averages for a variety of ratios. For example, fast-food companies would not be expected to have a large receivables balance.

The cash ratio is even stricter than the quick ratio and measure the ability of a company to pay its current liabilities with the cash and investments it has on hand.

$$\text{Cash ratio} = \frac{\text{Cash + Short-term investments}}{\text{Current liabilities}}$$

The cash ratio is useful if the collectibility of a company's accounts receivables is in doubt.

The operating cash flow ratio focuses on the company's ability to generate cash rather than focusing just on the cash existing at year end.

$$\text{Operating cash flow ratio} = \frac{\text{Cash flow from operations}}{\text{Current liabilities}}$$

Exhibit 3.2 summarizes the liquidity ratios and cash flow ratios discussed in this chapter. Exhibit 3.5 contains examples of these ratios for Duke Energy and Southern Company, for which financial statements are shown in Exhibits 3.3 and 3.4.

Cash Flow Ratios

The cash-flow-to-net-income ratio reflects the relationship between accrual-basis results of operations and cash-basis results of operations. So

EXHIBIT 3.2

Summary of Liquidity and Cash Flow Ratios

Liquidity Ratios			**Cash Flow Ratios**		
Current ratio	=	$\frac{\text{Current assets}}{\text{Current liabilities}}$	Cash flow to net income ratio	=	$\frac{\text{Cash from operations}}{\text{Net income}}$
Quick ratio	=	$\frac{\text{Cash + Investments + Accts. Receivable}}{\text{Current liabilities}}$	Cash flow adequacy ratio	=	$\frac{\text{Cash from operations}}{\text{Capital expenditures}}$
Cash ratio	=	$\frac{\text{Cash + Investments}}{\text{Current liabilities}}$	Cash flow adequacy ratio	=	$\frac{\text{Cash from operations}}{\text{Long-term debt}}$
Operating cash flow ratio	=	$\frac{\text{Cash flow from operations}}{\text{Currrent liabilities}}$	Cash times interest earned ratio	=	$\frac{\text{Cash from operations + Interest payments + Tax payment}}{\text{Cash paid for interest}}$

it is an important indication of the extent to which accrual-basis assumptions have affected net income.

$$\text{Cash-flow-to-net-income ratio} = \frac{\text{Cash from operations}}{\text{Net income}}$$

If the cash-flow-to-net-income ratio is greater than 1, it is most likely because of noncash expenses like depreciation and amortization, as well as revenues that are received before they are earned. Noncash

EXHIBIT 3.3

Duke Energy Corporation Financial Statements

Consolidated Statements of Cash Flows

Years Ended December 31,	**2001**	**2000**	**1999**
			(In millions)
Cash Flows From Operating Activities			
Net income	$ 1,898	$ 1,776	$ 1,507
Adjustments to reconcile net income to net cash provided by operating activities:			
Depreciation and amortization	1,450	1,348	1,151
Cumulative effect of change in accounting principle	96	—	—
Extraordinary gain, net of tax	—	—	(660)
Gain on sale of equity investment	—	(407)	—
Provision on NAWE's California receivables	—	110	—
Impairment charges	36	—	—
Injuries and damages accrual	—	—	800
Deferred income taxes	129	152	(210)
Purchased capacity levelization	156	138	104
Transition cost recoveries, net	—	82	95
(Increase) decrease in			
Net unrealized mark-to-market and hedging transactions	91	(464)	(24)
Receivables	3,166	(5,167)	(659)
Inventory	(192)	(100)	(89)
Other current assets	694	(796)	(138)
Increase (decrease) in			
Accounts payable	(3,545)	4,867	477
Taxes accrued	183	(439)	(57)

EXHIBIT 3.3

DUKE ENERGY CORPORATION

FINANCIAL STATEMENTS CONTINUED

Years Ended December 31,	2001	2000	1999
Interest accrued	28	64	32
Other current liabilities	297	1,116	73
Other, assets	351	175	221
Other, liabilities	(243)	(230)	61
Net cash provided by operating activities	4,595	2,225	2,684
Cash Flows From Investing Activities			
Capital expenditures, net of cash acquired	(5,930)	(4,568)	(5,291)
Investment expenditures	(1,093)	(966)	(596)
Proceeds from sale of subsidiaries and equity investment	—	400	1,900
Notes Receivable	201	(158)	83
Other	541	362	153
Net cash used in investing activities	(6,281)	(4,930)	(3,751)
Cash Flows From Financing Activities			
Proceeds from the issuance of			
Long-term debt	2,673	3,206	3,221
Guaranteed preferred beneficial interests in subordinated notes of Duke Energy Corporation or subsidiaries	—	—	484
Common stock and stock options	1,432	230	162
Payments for the redemption of			
Long-term debt	(1,298)	(1,191)	(1,505)
Preferred and preference stock	(33)	(33)	(20)
Net change in notes payable and commercial paper	(246)	1,484	58
Distributions to minority interests	(329)	(1,216)	—
Contributions from minority interests	—	1,116	—

EXHIBIT 3.3

DUKE ENERGY CORPORATION
FINANCIAL STATEMENTS CONTINUED

Years Ended December 31,	2001	2000	1999
Dividends paid	(871)	(828)	(822)
Other	26	(54)	22
Net cash provided by financing activities	1,354	2,714	1,600
Net (decrease) increase in cash and cash equivalents	(332)	9	533
Cash and cash equivalents at beginning of period	622	613	80
Cash and cash equivalents at end of period	$ 290	$ 622	$ 613
Supplemental Disclosures			
Cash paid for interest, net of amount capitalized	$ 733	$ 817	$ 541
Cash paid for income taxes	$ 770	$ 1,177	$ 732

See Notes to Consolidated Financial Statements.

Consolidated Balance Sheets

December 31,	2001	2000
	(In millions)	
ASSETS		
Current Assets (Note 1)		
Cash and cash equivalents (Note 7)	$ 290	$ 622
Receivables (Notes 1 and 7)	5,301	8,648
Inventory (Note 1)	1,017	739
Current portion of purchased capacity costs (Note 5)	160	149
Unrealized gains on mark-to-market and hedging transactions (Notes 1 and 7)	2,326	11,038

EXHIBIT 3.3

Duke Energy Corporation
Financial Statements continued

December 31,	2001	2000
Other	451	1,317
Total current assets	9,545	22,513
Investments and Other Assets		
Investments in affiliates (Note 8)	1,480	1,387
Nuclear decommissioning trust funds (Note 11)	716	717
Pre-funded pension costs (Note 18)	313	304
Goodwill, net of accumulated amortization (Notes 1 and 2)	1,730	1,566
Notes receivable	576	462
Unrealized gains on mark-to-market and hedging transactions (Notes 1 and 7)	3,117	4,218
Other	1,299	1,143
Total investments and other assets	9,231	9,797
Property, Plant and Equipment (Notes 1, 5, 9, 10 and 11)		
Cost	39,464	34,598
Less accumulated depreciation and amortization	11,049	10,146
Net property, plant and equipment	28,415	24,452
Regulatory Assets and Deferred Debits (Notes 1 and 4)		
Purchased capacity costs (Note 5)	189	356
Deferred debt expense	203	208
Regulatory asset related to income taxes	510	506
Other (Notes 4 and 15)	282	400
Total regulatory assets and deferred debits	1,184	1,470
Total Assets	$48,375	$58,232

(See notes to Consolidated Financial Statements.)

EXHIBIT 3.3

DUKE ENERGY CORPORATION
FINANCIAL STATEMENTS CONTINUED

December 31,	**2001**	**2000**
		(In millions)
LIABILITIES AND COMMON STOCKHOLDERS' EQUITY		
Current Liabilities		
Accounts payable	$ 4,231	$ 7,733
Notes payable and commercial paper (Notes 7 and 10)	1,603	1,826
Taxes accrued (Note 1)	443	261
Interest accrued	239	208
Current maturities of long-term debt and preferred stock (Notes 10 and 14)	274	470
Unrealized losses on mark-to-market and hedging transactions (Notes 1 and 7)	1,519	11,070
Other (Notes 1 and 15)	2,118	1,769
Total current liabilities	10,427	23,337
Long-term Debt (Notes 7 and 10)	12,321	10,717
Deferred Credits and Other Liabilities (Note 1)		
Deferred income taxes (Note 6)	4,307	3,851
Investment tax credit (Note 6)	189	211
Nuclear decommissioning costs externally funded (Note 11)	716	717
Environmental cleanup liabilities (Note 15)	85	100
Unrealized losses on mark-to-market and hedging transactions (Notes 1 and 7)	2,212	3,581
Other (Notes 4 and 15)	1,542	1,574
Total deferred credits and other liabilities	9,051	10,034
Commitments and Contingencies (Notes 5, 11 and 15)		
Guaranteed Preferred Beneficial Interests in Subordinated Notes of Duke Energy Corporation or Subsidiaries (Notes 7 and 12)	1,407	1,406

EXHIBIT 3.3

DUKE ENERGY CORPORATION
FINANCIAL STATEMENTS CONTINUED

December 31,	2001	2000
Minority Interest in Financing Subsidiary (Note 13)	1,025	1,025
Minority Interests (Note 2)	1,221	1,410
Preferred and Preference Stock (Notes 7 and 14)		
Preferred and preference stock with sinking fund requirements	25	38
Preferred and preference stock without sinking fund requirements	209	209
Total preferred and preference stock	234	247
Common Stockholders' Equity (Notes 1, 16 and 17)		
Common stock, no par, 2 billion shares authorized; 777 million and 739 million shares outstanding at December 31, 2001 and 2000, respectively	6,217	4,797
Retained earnings	6,292	5,379
Accumulated other comprehensive income (loss)	180	(120)
Total common stockholders' equity	12,689	10,056
Total Liabilities and Common Stockholders' Equity	$48,375	$58,232

(See notes to Consolidated Financial Statements.)

EXHIBIT 3.4

Southern Company Financial Statements (2001 Annual Report)

Consolidated Statements of Cash Flows

At December 31,	**2001**	**2000**	**1999**
			(in millions)
Operating Activities:			
Consolidated net income	$ 1,262	$ 1,313	$ 1,276
Adjustments to reconcile consolidated net income to net cash provided from operating activities—			
Less income from discontinued operations	142	319	361
Depreciation and amortization	1,358	1,337	1,216
Deferred income			
Taxes and investment			
Tax credits	(22)	97	10
Other, net	(192)	18	118
Changes in certain current assets and liabilities—			
Receivables, net	344	(379)	(141)
Fossil fuel stock	(199)	78	(41)
Materials and supplies	(43)	(15)	(37)
Accounts payable	(51)	180	(65)
Other	69	66	244
Net cash provided from operating activities of continuing operations	2,384	2,376	2,219
Investing Activities:			
Gross property additions	(2,617)	(2,225)	(1,881)
Other	(119)	(81)	(362)

EXHIBIT 3.4

SOUTHERN COMPANY FINANCIAL STATEMENTS CONTINUED

December 31,	2001	2000	1999
Net cash used for investing activities of continuing operations	(2,736)	(2,306)	(2,243)
Financing Activities:			
Increase (decrease) in notes payable, net	223	(275)	831
Proceeds—			
Long-term senior notes	1,242	650	840
Other long-term debt	757	93	629
Capital and preferred securities	30	–	250
Common stock	395	910	24
Redemptions—			
First mortgage bonds	(616)	(211)	(890)
Other long-term debt	(569)	(204)	(483)
Capital and preferred securities	–	–	(100)
Preferred stock	–	–	(86)
Common stock repurchased	–	(415)	(862)
Payment of common stock dividends	(922)	(873)	(921)
Other	(33)	(54)	(50)
Net cash provided from (used for) financing activities of continuing operations	507	(379)	(818)
Cash provided from (used for) discontinued operations	–	354	684
Net Increase (Decrease) in Cash and Cash Equivalents	155	45	(158)
Cash and Cash Equivalents at Beginning of Year	199	154	312
Cash and Cash Equivalents at End of Year	$ 354	$ 199	$ 154

EXHIBIT 3.4

SOUTHERN COMPANY FINANCIAL STATEMENTS CONTINUED

	2001	2000	1999
Supplemental Cash Flow Information			
From Continuing Operations:			
Cash paid during the year for—			
Interest (net of amount capitalized)	$624	$802	$684
Income taxes	$721	$666	$656

(The accompanying notes are an integral part of these statements.)

Consolidated Balance Sheets

Assets at December 31	**2001**	**2000**
	(in millions)	
Current Assets:		
Cash and cash equivalents	$ 354	$ 199
Special deposits	23	6
Receivables, less accumulated provisions for uncollectible accounts of $24 in 2001 and $22 in 2000	1,132	1,312
Under recovered retail fuel clause revenue	280	418
Fossil fuel stock, at average cost	394	195
Materials and supplies, at average cost	550	507
Other	223	188
Total current assets	2,956	2,825
Property, Plant and Equipment: In service	35,813	34,188
Less accumulated depreciation	15,020	14,350
	20,793	19,838
Nuclear fuel, at amortized cost	202	215
Construction work in progress	2,089	1,569

EXHIBIT 3.4

SOUTHERN COMPANY FINANCIAL STATEMENTS CONTINUED

	2001	2000
Total property, plant and equipment	23,084	21,622
Other Property and Investments:		
Nuclear decommissioning trusts, at fair value	682	690
Net assets of discontinued operations	–	3,320
Leveraged leases	655	596
Other	193	161
Total other property and investments	1,530	4,767
Deferred Charges and Other Assets:		
Deferred charges related to income taxes	924	957
Prepaid pension costs	547	398
Debt expense, being amortized	103	99
Premium on reacquired debt, being amortized	280	280
Other	400	312
Total deferred charges and other assets	2,254	2,046
Total Assets	$29,824	$31,260

(The accompanying notes are an integral part of these balance sheets.)

Liabilities and Stockholders' Equity	**2001**	**2000**
		(in millions)
Current Liabilities:		
Securities due within one year	$ 429	$ 67
Notes payable	1,902	1,680
Accounts payable	847	869
Customer deposits	153	140
Taxes accrued—		
Income taxes	160	88
Other	193	208
Interest accrued	118	121
Vacation pay accrued	125	119

EXHIBIT 3.4

Southern Company Financial Statements continued

	2001	2000
Other	445	426
Total current liabilities	4,372	3,718
Long-term debt (See accompanying statements)	8,297	7,843
Deferred Credits and Other Liabilities:		
Accumulated deferred income taxes	4,088	4,074
Deferred credits related to income taxes	500	551
Accumulated deferred investment tax credits	634	664
Employee benefits provisions	450	401
Prepaid capacity revenues	41	58
Other	814	647
Total deferred credits and other liabilities	6,527	6,395
Company or subsidiary obligated mandatorily redeemable capital and preferred securities (See accompanying statements)	2,276	2,246
Cumulative preferred stock of subsidiaries (See accompanying statements)	368	368
Common stockholders' equity (See accompanying statements)	7,984	10,690
Total Liabilities and Stockholders' Equity	$29,824	$31,260

Commitments and Contingent Matters (Notes 1, 2, 3, 5, 8, 9, and 10)

(The accompanying notes are an integral part of these balance sheets.)

Source: EDGARSCAN at PWCGlobal.com.

EXHIBIT 3.5

Ratio Comparison for Duke

Current ratio	=	$\frac{\text{Current assets}}{\text{Current liabilities}}$
Quick ratio	=	$\frac{\text{Quick assets}}{\text{Current liabilities}}$
Cash ratio	=	$\frac{\text{Cash + Short-term investments}}{\text{Current liabilities}}$
Operating cash flow ratio	=	$\frac{\text{Cash flow from operations}}{\text{Current liabilities}}$
Cash flow to net income	=	$\frac{\text{Cash from operations}}{\text{Net income}}$
Cash flow adequacy ratio	=	$\frac{\text{Cash from operations}}{\text{Expenditures for fixed asset additions and business acquisition}}$
Cash flow adequacy ratio	=	$\frac{\text{Cash from operations}}{\text{LT asset purchases + LT debt payments + Dividend payments}}$
Cash times interest earned	=	$\frac{\text{Cash for operations + Interest payments + tax payments}}{\text{Cash paid for interest}}$

Energy and Southern Company

	Duke Energy		Southern Company	
=	$\frac{\$9,545}{\$10,427}$	= 0.915	$\frac{\$2,956}{\$4,372}$	= 0.676
=	$\frac{\$290 + 5,301}{\$10,427}$	= 0.536	$\frac{\$354 + 23 + 1,132}{\$4,372}$	= 0.345
=	$\frac{\$290}{\$10,427}$	= 0.028	$\frac{\$354 + 23}{\$4,372}$	= 0.086
=	$\frac{\$4,595}{\$10,427}$	= 0.441	$\frac{\$2,384}{\$4,372}$	= 0.545
=	$\frac{\$4,595}{\$1,898}$	= 2.421	$\frac{\$2,384}{\$1,262}$	= 1.889
=	$\frac{\$4,595}{\$5,930}$	= 0.775	$\frac{\$2,384}{\$2,617}$	= 0.911
=	$\frac{\$4,595}{\$5,930 + 1,298 + 871}$	= 0.567	$\frac{\$2,384}{\$2,617 + 1,185 + 922}$	= 0.505
=	$\frac{\$4,595 + 733 + 770}{\$733}$	= 8.319	$\frac{\$2,384 + 624 + 721}{\$733 =}$	= 5.081

TIPS AND TECHNIQUES

The current and quick ratios indicate the ability of a company to settle current liabilities. However, these ratios are based on amounts reported in balance sheet accounts (e.g., cash, inventory). Companies may have access to cash in addition to the current assets reported, such as a revolving credit facility. This information would be in the notes to the financial statements.

expenses reduce net income but have no effect on cash flow. The bigger the ratio, the more accounting assumptions are impacting net income.

Cash Flow Adequacy Ratio

Cash flow adequacy refers to whether there is enough cash generated by a company's operations to pay for its investments in long-term assets such as its plant assets or equipment, and still have cash to pay off debt or distribute dividends. The equation basically relates operating activities to investing activities:

$$\text{Cash flow adequacy ratio} = \frac{\text{Cash from operations}}{\text{Expenditures for fixed asset additions and new business acquisitions}}$$

A cash flow adequacy ratio greater than 1 would indicate that a company's operations generate enough cash to grow the business. If the ratio is less than 1, then the company's operations are not able to pay for business growth, and other sources of financing are needed, from borrowing or from investors, simply to support the cash cost of operations.

Another version of the cash flow adequacy ratio broadens it to consider the adequacy of cash to cover not only investing activities but also some financing activities like debt repayment and dividend payments. The following equation basically relates operating activities to investing and financing activities.

TIPS AND TECHNIQUES

One way to imagine the practicality of the cash-flow-to-net-income ratio (or to remember it) is to examine the cash flow statement, particularly the cash from operations section. If it was prepared in the indirect method (which most companies in the United States use), then it begins with net income and ends with cash from operations, as follows:

Net income	$10,000
+ Depreciation expense	5,000
– Increase in accounts receivable	(2,000)
+ Decrease in inventory	4,000
– Decrease in accounts payable	(3,000)
Cash from operations	$14,000

Obviously, the cash-flow-to-net-income ratio is the end of that section divided by the beginning ($14,000 ÷ $10,000 = 1.40).

$$\text{Cash flow adequacy ratio} = \frac{\text{Cash from operations}}{\text{Long-term asset purchases} + \text{Long-term Debt repayments} + \text{Dividend payments}}$$

In the long run, operating activities must support financing and investing activities, not vice versa.

Cash Times Interest Earned

Creditors need to know whether borrowers can pay interest on their debt. Interest-paying ability can be shown by the cash times interest earned ratio.

$$\text{Cash times interest earned} = \frac{\text{Cash before interest and taxes}}{\text{Cash paid for interest}}$$

$$= \frac{\text{Cash from operations} + \text{interest payments} + \text{tax payments}}{\text{Cash paid for interest}}$$

The numerator represents pretax cash flow since interest is paid before taxes are calculated. The most important thing about this ratio is its trend over the years. A decrease could indicate trouble.

Solvency

Everyone with a financial stake in a company wants to know whether it will be successful or, in a worst case, even stay in business. Fortunately, analysts and bankers are working on finding out whether a company is a going concern. Auditors are responsible for assessing a company's going-concern status, but are not required to search out evidence of going-concern status. In the case of Enron, these groups did not get it right soon enough. But often they are able to evaluate a failing financial picture pretty accurately. A study by Barber, Lehavy, McNichols, and Trueman[1] showed that the most highly recommended stocks (of brokerage houses and analysts) overall produced average annual rates of return that were much higher than the least favorably recommended stocks. According to James Glassman, "an investor who bought the top-rated stocks and shorted the lowest-rated stocks would beat the market by about nine percentage points a year."[2] So keeping up with analysts' ratings is worthwhile.

Financial Leverage

The principle of obtaining an advantage using leverage is frequently discussed in a physics course. When a lever is properly placed across a fulcrum, downward pressure on the long end of the fulcrum results in a greatly magnified upward force on the short end. Ten pounds of downward pressure may be sufficient to lift a 100-pound weight. A small child may lift a large boulder. When a child lifts a rock with a lever, leverage gives the child a mechanical advantage.

Companies use leverage to increase both their return on assets (ROA) and their return on owners' equity (ROE). There are two types of leverage: operational leverage to increase ROA and financial leverage to increase ROE. Both are similar to mechanics, only operational and financial leverage (FL) magnify the strength of dollar and cents inputs. The three basic types of leverage are listed with their properties in Exhibit 3.6.

FL is the use of debt instead of or in addition to owners' investment as a source of capital. The right amount of leverage (the right mix of creditor and owner financing) can affect the company favorably. Too much debt can be unfavorable. The presence of debt increases a company's risk and thus its cost of additional capital, but may also increase its ROE. This can be illustrated with the following example of two companies with the same total assets and the same net income but different relative amounts of debt and owner investment.

EXHIBIT 3.6

Three Types of Leverage

Type of Leverage	Nature of the Advantage	Use
Physical leverage	Mechanical	To increase strength in lifting
Financial leverage	Capital structure	To increase return on equity *
Operating leverage	Asset mix	To increase return on investment **

$$* \text{ ROE} = \frac{\text{Earnings}}{\text{Common stockholders' equity}}$$

$$** \text{ ROA} = \frac{\text{Earnings}}{\text{Investment in assets}}$$

	Company A	Company B
Balance Sheet		
Assets	$100,000	$100,000
Liabilities	40,000	60,000
Owners' equity	60,000	40,000
Income Statement		
Net income	10,000	10,000

The ROE model is summarized as follows:

$$\text{ROE} = \text{ROA} \times \text{FL}$$

$$\text{Return on equity} = \text{Return on assets} \times \text{Financial leverage}$$

$$\frac{\text{Net income}}{\text{Equity}} = \frac{\text{Net income}}{\text{Assets}} \times \frac{\text{Assets}}{\text{Equity}}$$

Results for the two companies would look as follows:

		Company A	Company B
ROE =	$\frac{\text{Net income}}{\text{Equity}}$	$= \frac{\$10,000}{\$60,000} = 0.167$	$= \frac{\$10,000}{\$40,000} = 0.250$
ROA =	$\frac{\text{Net income}}{\text{Assets}}$	$= \frac{\$10,000}{\$100,000} = 0.10$	$= \frac{\$10,000}{\$100,000} = 0.10$
FL =	$\frac{\text{Assets}}{\text{Equity}}$	$= \frac{\$100,000}{\$60,000} = 1.67$	$= \frac{\$100,000}{\$40,000} = 2.50$

Company B has more FL, as shown by a higher number for debt and a higher FL ratio. Since both companies have a positive ROA, the ROE for both companies is magnified, with Company B's magnified to a greater extent due to the presence of more leverage.

This analysis compares two companies when they have the same net income and assets but different debt. The next section will examine the potential impact on both ROA and ROE when one company is faced with a choice between financing alternatives.

FL increases ROE by altering a company's capital structure or debt to owners' equity mix. In the following example, assume that investors are forming a company that requires assets of $5 million and is expected to produce earnings of $400,000 per year. If owners supply the entire $5 million, both the ROA and the ROE will be 8 percent (400,000/5 million). But what if owners borrowed half of the $5 million investment, and funds are available at 6 percent interest. If owners follow this route, investing $2.5 million and borrowing $2.5 million at 6 percent interest, earnings will be reduced by the $150,000 interest on the borrowed funds ($2.5 million × .06) reducing profits to $250,000.

Earnings before interest	$400,000
Interest	150,000
Earnings when owners borrow	$250,000

FL is concerned with ROE. Using the assumptions described, ROE is calculated under the two alternatives, no debt and debt at 6 percent interest:

	No Leverage	**Leverage**
Owners' investment	$5,000,000	$2,500,000
Debt	0	$2,500,000
Earnings	$ 400,000	$ 250,000
Total investment in assets	$5,000,000	$5,000,000
ROA	8%	5%
ROE	8%	10%

When owners borrow, the lower earnings (after interest expense) reduces the ROA, but because owners have invested less and have earned a rate of return on assets greater than the interest rate, ROE is increased.

Negative Financial Leverage

A company with any debt is using leverage. The greater the proportion of debt, the greater the leverage. A major decision centers on just how great a proportion of a company's funding should come from debt and how much from owners. The greater the debt, the greater the risk. Increased business risk results in higher interest rates on borrowed funds.

High Interest Rates. When interest rates are high—relative to the return on assets—FL may be detrimental. For instance, in the example above, assume that the owners decided to use financial leverage by borrowing $2.5 million, but that interest rates rose to 10 percent. If the business earns $400,000 before interest, the profit after an interest expense of $250,000 ($2.5 million × .10) will be only $150,000, and the return on owners' equity will be only 6 percent ($150,000/$2.5 million).

Earnings before interest	$400,000
Interest	$250,000
Earnings when owners borrow	$150,000

The following results are obtained under the two alternatives, no debt and debt at 10 percent interest:

	No Leverage	Leverage
Owners' investment	$5,000,000	$2,500,000
Earnings	$ 400,000	$ 150,000
Total asset investment	$5,000,000	$5,000,000
ROA	8%	3%
ROE	8%	6%

Low Earnings. If a company borrows money and conditions change so that earnings are less than expected, ROE is adversely affected. Assume that the company borrowed funds as planned at 10 percent, but conditions changed and the company earned only $300,000 before the interest charges. After paying the $250,000 interest on the debt, profits would be only $50,000 and the return on owners' equity would be only 2 percent ($50,000/$2.5 million). If owners had not borrowed at all, the return on owners' equity would have been 6 percent ($300,000/$5 million).

Earnings before interest	$300,000
Interest	$250,000
Earnings when owners borrow	$ 50,000

The following results are obtained with low earnings under the two alternatives, no debt and debt at 10 percent interest:

	No Leverage	Leverage
Owners' investment	$5,000,000	$2,500,000
Earnings	$ 300,000	$ 50,000
Total asset investment	$5,000,000	$5,000,000
ROI	6%	1%
ROE	6%	2%

Financial leverage can be beneficial when times are good and risky when times are bad.

Other Measures of Leverage

The two debt-to-equity measures convey the same information as the financial leverage ratio (i.e., assets to equity). They are all about the relationships among the elements in the accounting equation

$$\text{Assets} = \text{Liabilities} + \text{Owners' equity}$$

When the assets-to-equity ratio is high (signifying a lot of debt), then the debt-to-equity ratios are high, too. As mentioned earlier, the right amount of debt for a company depends on the circumstances, like what debt-to-equity amounts are typical for the industry or what amounts may be included in debt covenants. Exhibit 3.7 shows some debt-to-equity results in May 2002 for two companies in the retail industry and two companies in the electric utilities industry.

Altman Z-score Model

A distress prediction model (or credit-scoring model) can be useful to a financial statement user who has financial statements but no access to the conference calls and such that bankers, brokers, and analysts are privy to. One of the well-known models is the Altman Z-score model:[3]

$$Z = .717(x_1) + .847(x_2) + 3.11(x_3) + .420(x_4) + .998(x_5)$$

Where x_1 = Net working capital/Total assets

x_2 = Retained earnings/Total assets
x_3 = EBIT/Total assets
x_4 = Shareholders' equity/Total liabilities
x_5 = Sales/Total assets

If Z is less than 1.20, then bankruptcy may follow. If Z is between 1.20 and 2.90, then the company's score is in the gray area.[4] So low values for the five ratios in the model would be bad news.

Net working capital to total assets (x_1) is the aspect of the model that reflects liquidity (recall that working capital is current assets minus current liabilities). Companies that have serious liquidity problems are the ones that sometimes file for bankruptcy protection to work out some arrangement with the creditors that will enable the company to make their payments to the creditors under a little more favorable arrangements. A low proportion of liquid assets to total assets could be problematic for the company.

Retained earnings to total assets (x_2) would be low for companies that have not accumulated much retained earnings over the years (sig-

EXHIBIT 3.7

Debt to Equity

		Company		Industry		S&P 500	
Company	Industry	Long-term debt to equity	Total debt to equity	Long-term debt to equity	Total debt to equity	Long-term debt to equity	Total debt to equity
Kmart	Retail	0.72	0.80	0.71	0.88	0.67	1.05
Wal-Mart	Retail	0.51	0.63	0.71	0.88	0.67	1.05
Southern	Electric	1.10	1.36	1.52	1.84	0.67	1.05
Duke	Electric	1.21	1.42	1.52	1.84	0.67	1.05

Source: Multex.com.

naling a pattern of lack of profitability or maybe an erosion of retained earnings due to recent net losses).

EBIT to total assets (x_3) is basically an ROA measure. Companies that declare bankruptcy are more likely to have had low earnings.

Shareholders' equity to total liabilities (x_4), if low, reflects the fact that the company has a relatively high amount of debt—usually a bad situation for an unprofitable company.

Sales to total assets (x_5) would be low for companies that are not effectively using their assets to produce sales.

Exhibits 3.8 through 3.10 show Z-scores for Duke Energy and Southern Company for the most recent year, and for Wal-Mart and Kmart for the years 2000 and 2001. It is interesting to note that Kmart's Z-scores, while obviously deteriorating, would not necessarily have predicted bankruptcy before it actually occurred. In fact, the bankruptcy filing, made in January 2002, seems to have caused a delay in the filing of

IN THE REAL WORLD

Beyond the Current Ratio

The current ratio is a traditional way to assess liquidity. If the current ratio (= current assets ÷ current liabilities) is greater than 1, then we know the company has at least $1.00 in current assets for every dollar of current liabilities. Some financial analysts look beyond what is in the balance sheet, to what is waiting in the wings. For example, Bill Gross, manager of the world's largest bond fund, was wary of General Electric in early 2002 because GE Capital had "commercial paper outstanding adding up to three times the size of the company's lines of credit with its banks." According to Gross, GE was "using near-hedge fund leverage."

Source: "Bond Heavyweight, Bill Gross, Slaps GE Over Disclosure, Debt Load," *The Wall Street Journal*, March 21, 2002.

EXHIBIT 3.8

Altman's Z-Score: Duke Company

At December 31, 2001 (in millions)

$$x_1 = \frac{\text{Net working capital}}{\text{Total assets}} = \frac{\$9{,}545 - \$10{,}427}{\$48{,}375} = -0.0182$$

$$x_2 = \frac{\text{Retained earnings}}{\text{Total assets}} = \frac{\$6{,}292}{\$48{,}375} = 0.1301$$

$$x_3 = \frac{\text{EBIT}}{\text{Total assets}} = \frac{\$4{,}100}{\$48{,}375} = 0.0848$$

$$x_4 = \frac{\text{Shareholders' equity}}{\text{Total liabilities}} = \frac{\$234 + \$12{,}689}{\$35{,}452} = 0.3645$$

$$x_5 = \frac{\text{Sales}}{\text{Total assets}} = \frac{\$57{,}780}{\$48{,}375} = 1.1944$$

For December 31, 2001:

$$Z = .717(x_1) + .847(x_2) + 3.11(x_3) + .420(x_4) + .998(x_5)$$

$$= .717(-0.0182) + .847(0.1301) + 3.11(0.0848) + .420(0.3645) + .998(1.1944)$$

$$= -0.0130 + 0.1102 + 0.2637 + 0.1531 + 1.1920$$

$$= 1.706$$

Conclusion: Duke is within the gray area of 1.20 to 2.90.

EXHIBIT 3.9

Altman's Z-Score: Southern Company

At December 31, 2001 (in millions)

$$x_1 = \frac{\text{Net working capital}}{\text{Total assets}} = \frac{\$2,956 - \$4,372}{\$29,824} = -0.0475$$

$$x_2 = \frac{\text{Retained earnings}}{\text{Total assets}} = \frac{\$4,517}{\$29,824} = 0.1515$$

$$x_3 = \frac{\text{EBIT}}{\text{Total assets}} = \frac{\$11,019}{\$29,824} = 0.0812$$

$$x_4 = \frac{\text{Shareholders' equity}}{\text{Total liabilities}} = \frac{\$7,984 + \$368}{\$21,472} = 0.3890$$

$$x_5 = \frac{\text{Sales}}{\text{Total assets}} = \frac{\$10,155}{\$29,824} = 0.3405$$

For December 31, 2001:

$$Z = .717(x_1) + .847(x_2) + 3.11(x_3) + .420(x_4) + .998(x_5)$$

$$= .717(-0.0475) + .847(0.1515) + 3.11(0.0812) + .420(0.3890) + .998(0.3405)$$

$$= -0.0341 + 0.1283 + 0.2525 + 0.1634 + 0.3398$$

$$= 0.8499$$

Conclusion: Southern Company is below the gray area of 1.20 to 2.90.

EXHIBIT 3.10

Altman's Z-Score: Wal-Mart

At January 31, 2001 (in millions)

$$x_1 = \frac{\text{Net working capital}}{\text{Total assets}}$$

$$= \frac{\$26{,}555 - \$28{,}949}{\$78{,}130} = \frac{-\$2{,}394}{\$78{,}130} = -0.0306$$

$$x_2 = \frac{\text{Retained earnings}}{\text{Total assets}}$$

$$= \frac{\$30{,}169}{\$78{,}130} = 0.3861$$

$$x_3 = \frac{\text{EBIT}}{\text{Total assets}}$$

$$= \frac{\$6{,}295 + \$1{,}374 + \$3{,}350}{\$78{,}130} = \frac{\$11{,}019}{\$78{,}130} = 0.1410$$

$$x_4 = \frac{\text{Shareholders' equity}}{\text{Total liabilities}}$$

$$= \frac{\$31{,}343}{\$46{,}787} = 0.6699$$

$$x_5 = \frac{\text{Sales}}{\text{Total assets}}$$

$$= \frac{\$191{,}329}{\$\ 78{,}130} = 2.4489$$

At January 31, 2001 (for fiscal year 2000):

$Z = .717(x_1) + .847(x_2) + 3.11(x_3) + .420(x_4) + .998(x_5)$

$= .717(-0.0306) + .847(0.3861) + 3.11(0.1410) + .420(0.6699) + .998(2.4489)$

$= -0.0219 + 0.3270 + 0.4385 + 0.2814 + 2.4440 = 3.4690$

At January 31, 2002 (for fiscal year 2001):

$Z = .717(x_1) + .847(x_2) + 3.11(x_3) + .420(x_4) + .998(x_5)$

$= .717(0.0116) + .847(0.4127) + 3.11(0.1403) + .420(0.7260) + .998(2.610)$

$= 0.0083 + 0.3496 + 0.4363 + 0.3049 + 2.6048 = 3.7039$

Conclusion: Wal-Mart is above the gray area of 1.20 to 2.90.

At January 31, 2002 (in millions)

$$\frac{\$28{,}246 - \$27{,}282}{\$83{,}451} = \frac{\$964}{\$83{,}451} = 0.0116$$

$$\frac{\$34{,}441}{\$83{,}451} = 0.4127$$

$$\frac{\$6{,}671 + \$1{,}326 + \$3{,}712}{\$83{,}451} = \frac{\$11{,}709}{\$83{,}451} = 0.1403$$

$$\frac{\$35{,}102}{\$48{,}349} = 0.7260$$

$$\frac{\$217{,}799}{\$83{,}451} = 2.610$$

EXHIBIT 3.10

Altman's Z-Score: Kmart

	At January 31, 2001		At January 31, 2002	
				(In millions)
$x_1 = \frac{\text{Net working capital}}{\text{Total assets}}$				
	$= \frac{\$7{,}884 - \$624}{\$14{,}298}$	$= 0.5078$	$\frac{\$7{,}752 - \$4{,}001}{\$14{,}832}$	$= 0.2529$
$x_2 = \frac{\text{Retained earnings}}{\text{Total assets}}$				
	$= \frac{\$1{,}261}{\$14{,}298}$	$= 0.0882$	$\frac{\$4{,}018}{\$14{,}832}$	$= 0.2709$
$x_3 = \frac{\text{EBIT}}{\text{Total assets}}$				
	$= \frac{(\$2{,}472)}{\$14{,}298}$	$= -0.1729$	$\frac{(\$45)}{\$14{,}832}$	$= -0.0030$
$x_4 = \frac{\text{Shareholders' equity}}{\text{Total liabilities}}$				
	$= \frac{\$4{,}348}{\$9{,}950}$	$= 0.4370$	$\frac{\$6{,}970}{\$7{,}862}$	$= 0.8865$
$x_5 = \frac{\text{Sales}}{\text{Total assets}}$				
	$= \frac{\$36{,}151}{\$14{,}298}$	$= 2.5284$	$\frac{\$37{,}028}{\$14{,}832}$	$= 2.4965$

At January 31, 2001 (for fiscal year 2000):

$Z = .717(x_1) + .847(x_2) + 3.11(x_3) + .420(x_4) + .998(x_5)$

$= .717(0.2529) + .847(0.2709) + 3.11(-0.0030) + .420(0.8865) + .998(2.4965)$

$= 0.1813 + 0.2295 + (-0.0093) + 0.3723 + 2.4915 = 3.2653$

At January 31, 2002 (for fiscal year 2001):

$Z = .717(x_1) + .847(x_2) + 3.11(x_3) + .420(x_4) + .998(x_5)$

$= .717(0.5078) + .847(0.0882) + 3.11(-0.1729) + .420(0.4370) + .998(2.5284)$

$= 0.3641 + 0.0747 + (-0.5377) + 0.1835 + 2.5233 = 2.6079$

Conclusion: Kmart is above the gray area of 1.20 to 2.90 for fiscal year 2000 but within the gray area for fiscal year 2001.

the 10K with the Securities and Exchange Commission (SEC) since that filing was not made until May 2002, for the fiscal year ending January 31, 2002. Financial statements for Wal-Mart and Kmart are shown in Exhibits 3.11 and 3.12.

EXHIBIT 3.11

WalMart Stores Inc. Financial Statements

Consolidated Balance Sheets

January 31,	**2002**	**2001**
	(in millions)	
Assets		
Current Assets		
Cash and cash equivalents	$ 2,161	$ 2,054
Receivables	2,000	1,768
Inventories		
At replacement cost	22,749	21,644
Less LIFO reserve	135	202
Inventories at LIFO cost	22,614	21,442
Prepaid expenses and other	1,471	1,291
Total Current Assets	28,246	26,555
Property, Plant and Equipment, at Cost		
Land	10,241	9,433
Building and improvements	28,527	24,537
Fixtures and equipment	14,135	12,964
Transportation equipment	1,089	879
	53,992	47,813
Less accumulated depreciation	11,436	10,196
Net property, plant and equipment	42,556	37,617
Property under Capital Lease		
Property under capital lease	4,626	4,620
Less accumulated amortization	1,432	1,303
Net property under capital leases	3,194	3,317

EXHIBIT 3.11

WALMART STORES INC. FINANCIAL STATEMENTS CONTINUED

January 31,	2002	2001
		(in millions)
Other Assets and Deferred Charges		
Net goodwill and other acquired intangible assets	8,595	9,059
Other assets and deferred charges	860	1,582
Total Assets	$ 83,451	$ 78,130
Liabilities and Shareholders Equity		
Current Liabilities		
Commercial paper	$ 743	$ 2,286
Accounts payable	15,617	15,092
Accrued liabilities	7,174	6,355
Accrued income taxes	1,343	841
Long-term debt due within one year	2,257	4,234
Obligations under capital leases due within one year	148	141
Total Current Liabilities	27,282	28,949
Long-Term Debt	15,687	12,501
Long-Term Obligations Under Capital Leases	3,045	3,154
Deferred Income Taxes and Other	1,128	1,043
Minority Interest	1,207	1,140
Shareholders Equity		
Preferred stock ($0.10 par value; 100 shares authorized, none issued)		
Common stock ($0.10 par value; 11,000 shares authorized, 4,453 and 4,470 issued and outstanding in 2002 and 2001, respectively)	445	447
Capital in excess of par value	1,484	1,411
Retained earnings	34,441	30,169
Other accumulated comprehensive income	(1,268)	(684)
Total Shareholders Equity	35,102	31,343
Total Liabilities and Shareholders Equity	$ 83,451	$ 78,130

(See accompanying notes.)

EXHIBIT 3.11

WALMART STORES INC. FINANCIAL STATEMENTS CONTINUED

Consolidated Statements of Cash Flows

Fiscal years ended January 31,	2002	2001	2000
			(in millions)
Cash flows from operating activities			
Net Income	$ 6,671	$ 6,295	$ 5,377
Adjustments to reconcile net income to net cash provided by operating activities:			
Depreciation and amortization	3,290	2,868	2,375
Cumulative effect of accounting change, net of tax			198
Increase in accounts receivable	(210)	(422)	(255)
Increase in inventories	(1,235)	(1,795)	(2,088)
Increase in accounts payable	368	2,061	1,849
Increase in accrued liabilities	1,125	11	1,015
Deferred income taxes	185	342	(138)
Other	66	244	(139)
Net cash provided by operating activities	10,260	9,604	8,194
Cash flows from investing activities			
Payments for property, plant and equipment	(8,383)	(8,042)	(6,183)
Investment in international operations (net of cash acquired, $195 million in Fiscal 2000)		(627)	(10,419)
Proceeds from termination of net investment hedges	1,134		
Other investing activities	103	(45)	(244)
Net cash used in investing activities	(7,146)	(8,714)	(16,846)
Cash flows from financing activities			
Increase/(decrease) in commercial paper	(1,533)	(2,022)	4,316
Proceeds from issuance of long-term debt	4,591	3,778	6,000

EXHIBIT 3.11

WALMART STORES INC. FINANCIAL STATEMENTS CONTINUED

Fiscal years ended January 31,	2002	2001	2000
Purchase of company stock	(1,214)	(193)	(101)
Dividends paid	(1,249)	(1,070)	(890)
Payment of long-term debt	(3,519)	(1,519)	(863)
Payment of capital lease obligations	(167)	(173)	(133)
Proceeds from issuance of company stock		581	
Other financing activities	113	176	224
Net cash provided by (used in) financing activities	(2,978)	(442)	8,553
Effect of exchange rate changes on cash	(29)	(250)	76
Net increase/(decrease) in cash and cash equivalents	107	198	(23)
Cash and cash equivalents at beginning of year	2,054	1,856	1,879
Cash and cash equivalents at end of year	$ 2,161	$ 2,054	$ 1,856
Supplemental disclosure of cash flow information			
Income tax paid	$ 3,196	$ 3,509	$ 2,780
Interest paid	1,312	1,319	849
Capital lease obligations incurred	225	576	378
Property, plant and equipment acquired with debt			65
ASDA acquisition cost satisfied with debt			264
ASDA acquisition cost satisfied with company stock			175

(See accompanying notes.)

Source: EDGARSCAN at PWCGlobal.COM.

EXHIBIT 3.12

Kmart Financial Statements

Consolidated Balance Sheets

	January 30, 2001	January 31, 2000
	(in millions, except share data)	
ASSETS		
CURRENT ASSETS		
Cash and cash equivalents	$ 1,245	$ 401
Merchandise inventories	5,822	6,412
Other current assets	817	939
TOTAL CURRENT ASSETS	7,884	7,752
Property and equipment, net	6,161	6,557
Other assets and deferred charges	253	523
TOTAL ASSETS	$14,298	$14,832
LIABILITIES AND SHAREHOLDERS' EQUITY		
CURRENT LIABILITIES		
Long-term debt due within one year	$ —	$ 68
Accounts payable	103	2,159
Accrued payroll and other liabilities	378	1,587
Taxes other than income taxes	143	187
TOTAL CURRENT LIABILITIES	624	4,001
Long-term debt and notes payable	330	2,084
Capital lease obligations	857	943
Other long-term liabilities	79	834
TOTAL LIABILITIES NOT SUBJECT TO COMPROMISE	1,890	7,862
Liabilities subject to compromise	8,060	—
Company obligated mandatorily redeemable convertible preferred securities of a subsidiary trust holding solely 7¾% convertible junior subordinated debentures of Kmart (redemption value of $898 and $898, respectively)	889	887

EXHIBIT 3.12

KMART FINANCIAL STATEMENTS CONTINUED

	January 30, 2001	January 31, 2000
Common stock, $1 par value, 1,500,000,000 shares authorized; 503,294,515 and 486,509,736 shares issued, respectively	503	487
Capital in excess of par value	1,695	1,578
Retained earnings	1,261	4,018
TOTAL LIABILITIES AND SHAREHOLDERS' EQUITY	$14,298	$14,832

(See accompanying Notes to Consolidated Financial Statements.)

Consolidated Statements of Cash Flows

	January 30, 2001	January 31, 2000	January 26, 1999
			(in millions)
CASH FLOWS FROM OPERATING ACTIVITIES			
Net income (loss) from continuing operations	$(2,587)	$ (244)	$ 633
Adjustments to reconcile net income (loss) from continuing operations to net cash provided by operating activities:			
Restructuring, impairment and other charges	1,262	728	—
Reorganization items	(184)	—	—
Depreciation and amortization	824	777	770
Equity (income) loss in unconsolidated subsidiaries	—	13	(44)
Dividends received from Meldisco	51	44	38
Decrease (increase) in inventories	596	324	(565)
Increase (decrease) in accounts payable	996	(145)	168
Deferred income taxes and taxes payable	(55)	(204)	258
Changes in other assets	222	48	(105)

EXHIBIT 3.12

KMART FINANCIAL STATEMENTS CONTINUED

	January 30, 2001	January 31, 2000	January 26, 1999
Changes in other liabilities	102	(10)	94
Cash used for store closings	(128)	(102)	(80)
Net cash provided by continuing operations	1,099	1,229	1,167
Net cash used for discontinued operations	(102)	(115)	(83)
NET CASH PROVIDED BY OPERATING ACTIVITIES	997	1,114	1,084
NET CASH USED FOR REORGANIZATION ITEMS	(6)	—	—
CASH FLOWS FROM INVESTING ACTIVITIES			
Capital expenditures	(1,456)	(1,089)	(1,277)
Investment in BlueLight.com	(45)	(55)	—
Acquisition of Caldor leases	—	—	(86)
NET CASH USED FOR INVESTING ACTIVITIES	(1,501)	(1,144)	(1,363)
CASH FLOWS FROM FINANCING ACTIVITIES			
Proceeds from issuance of debt	1,824	400	300
Debt issuance costs	(49)	(3)	(3)
Issuance of common shares	56	53	63
Purchase of convertible preferred securities of subsidiary trust	—	(84)	—
Purchase of common shares	—	(55)	(200)
Payments on debt	(320)	(73)	(90)
Payments on capital lease obligations	(85)	(78)	(77)
Payments of dividends on preferred securities of subsidiary trust	(72)	(73)	(80)
NET CASH PROVIDED BY (USED FOR) FINANCING ACTIVITIES	1,354	87	(87)

EXHIBIT 3.12

KMART FINANCIAL STATEMENTS CONTINUED

	2001	2000	1999
NET CHANGE IN CASH AND CASH EQUIVALENTS	844	57	(366)
CASH AND CASH EQUIVALENTS, BEGINNING OF YEAR	401	344	710
CASH AND CASH EQUIVALENTS, END OF YEAR	$ 1,245	$ 401	$ 344

(See accompanying notes to Consolidated Financial Statements.)

The important thing to remember is that the Z-score may serve as a red flag, not a scientific fact of impending demise. Examine the values of the components of Altman's model for companies relative to their industries. If anything is way out of line, consider the company's circumstances. If the company is heading into a cash crunch, is not profitable, and has a lot of debt, there is trouble ahead.

Off-Balance-Sheet Debt

The publicity surrounding Enron and Adelphia practically made off-balance-sheet debt a household term. In a very broad sense, off-balance-sheet debt exists when a company makes a commitment for something or a guarantee of something without actually recording a liability. In a somewhat narrower sense, off-balance-sheet debt exists when a company sets up an organization through which it can obtain financing without actually having to borrow the cash directly. Motivations for setting up such an arrangement include the desire to manage earnings or financial reporting in general and/or the desire to manage risk or the appearance

TIPS AND TECHNIQUES

Debt Covenants

Debt covenants can hang over a company like a dark cloud because debt covenants can make all the difference in a company's future. For example, very early in 2002, Qwest Communications International, Inc., was working hard to reduce debt and expenses in order to avoid being in violation of certain debt covenants by that summer. One of the covenants required that debt not be more than 3.75 times earnings before interest, taxes, depreciation, and amortization (EBITDA). Violation of a debt covenant can lead to loss of credit, which can lead to bankruptcy. Interested financial statement users and other parties should try to find out a company's debt covenants or at least those that are typical for the industry as a benchmark against which to evaluate a company's situation.

of risk. As this chapter shows, investors and creditors look closely at the amount of debt a company has in order to ascertain how much risk the company might be exposed to. A company's "borrowing" money without looking like it is borrowing money could be seen as a necessary objective by a company's management.

That is not to say that these arrangements are not legitimate means for achieving some goals. In fact, there is guidance for achieving certain objectives with these special-purpose entities (SPEs). An SPE, which can be in the form of a corporation, partnership, limited liability company, or trust, is created to fulfill a certain purpose. Some companies have used SPEs to generate financing; some companies have used SPEs by transferring certain assets to them or by creating certain tax advantages through them. One of the accounting issues that has backfired against companies using SPEs is how to let the public know about the SPE.

IN THE REAL WORLD

Disclosure of Debt-Rating Triggers

According to Alan Levinsohn, finance editor of *Strategic Finance*, "The biggest overall change in annual reports this year is disclosure of debt-rating triggers of financing arrangements."* Such triggers require immediate payment of a loan if the company's debt rating falls. Enron's and Kmart's situations were made worse by situations like this. An example of this type of disclosure is included in the Management's Discussion and Analysis section of GE's annual report for 2001:

> PRINCIPAL DEBT CONDITIONS that could automatically result in remedies, such as acceleration of GE or GECS debt, are described below.
>
> - If the short-term credit rating of GE Capital or certain special purpose entities previously discussed were to fall below. A–1+/P–1, GE Capital would be required to provide substitute liquidity for those entities or to purchase the outstanding commercial paper. The maximum amount that GE Capital would be required to provide in the event of such a downgrade is $43.2 billion at December 31, 2001.
> - If the long-term credit rating of GE Capital or certain special purpose entities previously discussed were to fall below AA–/Aa3, GE Capital would be required to provide substitute credit support or liquidate the special purpose entities. The maximum amount that GE Capital would be required to substitute in the event of such a downgrade is $14.5 billion at December 31, 2001.
> - If the long-term credit rating of either GE or GECS under certain swap, forward and option contracts falls below A–/A3, certain remedies are required as discussed in note 29.

IN THE REAL WORLD CONTINUED

- If GE Capital's ratio of earnings to fixed charges, which was 1.72 to 1 at the end of 2001 deteriorates to 1.10 to 1 or, upon redemption of certain preferred stock, its ratio of debt to equity, which was 7.31 to 1 at the end of 2001 exceeds 8 to 1, GE has committed to contribute capital to GE Capital. GE also has guaranteed subordinated debt of GECS with a face amount of $1.0 billion at December 31, 2001, and 2000.
- If the GE long-term credit rating were to fall below investment grade (a downgrade of 9 ratings increments), certain special purpose entities with which GE has financing arrangements would have the right to terminate those arrangements potentially requiring $2.5 billion of secured funding.

None of these conditions has been met in GE or GECS history, and management believes that under any reasonable future economic developments, the likelihood is remote that any such arrangements could have a significant effect on GE and GECS operations, cash flows or financial position.

TIMING OF CONTRACTUAL COMMITMENTS at GE and GECS, related to leases and debt, follow.

In Billions	2002	2003	2004	2005	2006
GE	$ 2.2	$ 0.5	$ 0.5	$ 0.3	$ 0.3
GECS					
Commercial paper	117.5	—	—	—	—
Other	44.4	26.4	15.2	10.5	6.9

Source: GE Annual Report 2001.

*See Alan Levinsohn, "Trends in Financial Management: A Scramble to Self-Regulate," *Strategic Finance*, May 2002, 63.

IN THE REAL WORLD

Off-Balance Sheet Financing and Material Adverse Change Clauses

So much of a company's future can be caught up in its debt and the arrangements surrounding the debt agreements. A thorough financial analysis should involve examining a company's debt, whether on the balance sheet or off of it, and, if possible, any details about the material adverse change clauses in the provisions for the debt. Such clauses contain the triggers that will require immediate repayment of the debt. For example, Enron used partnerships (special-purpose vehicles) to help get debt off Enron's balance sheet. There were provisions in the debt that required repayment in stock of the parent company (Enron) if its credit was downgraded and stock prices went below certain levels. For Enron, both triggers "were set off."

Source: Randall Smith and Jathon Sapsford, "Debt Triggers Spark Worries Due to Enron," *The Wall Street Journal,* February 15, 2002, C1, C8.

There are three ways to report the existence or use of an SPE by a sponsoring company:

1. Consolidate the SPE by including all assets and liabilities of the SPE on the balance sheet of the sponsoring company.
2. Recognize a liability in the balance sheet, for whatever obligation arises from the use of the SPE.
3. Disclose the obligation in the footnotes to the financial statements.

In general, a sponsoring company has to consolidate the SPE unless some other independent third party has a controlling interest in the SPE and that interest is equal to at least 3 percent of the total assets. For example, if an SPE has assets equal to $100,000, financed with $97,000 in debt

IN THE REAL WORLD

In May 2002, Standard and Poor's (S&P) published a report on companies facing a cash shortfall. S&P compiled a list, including some very recognizable name (like Dynegy, Reliant Resources, Tyco International, and Georgia Pacific) of companies that "could face severe problems if their debt is downgraded, or if certain clauses in their financial agreements are breached." This was a first for S&P and is an apparent response to growing concern about companies' financial statements and credit agencies' failure to alert the public to impending liquidity problems. Enron had been listed as investment grade until just days before its bankruptcy filing.

S&P studied 950 U.S. and European investment-grade companies and found that 23 of them were vulnerable to debt triggers like credit-rating downgrades, stock price drops, and earnings downturns. Debt triggers can suddenly necessitate coming up with huge amounts of cash for loan collateral or even loan payoffs, so they can spark a liquidity crisis. A liquidity crisis can spark an investor-confidence crisis, which adversely affects stock prices, which adversely affects the company's ability to raise additional capital. S&P's apparent objective is to better inform the public about the possibilities.

Source: Gregory Zuckerman and Mitchell Benson, "S&P Draws Up List of Firms that May Face Cash Shortfall," *The Wall Street Journal*, May 16, 2002.

and $3,000 from an independent third-party owner, the sponsoring company would not consolidate. If the SPE's assets are financed with $95,000 in debt, $3,000 from the third-party owners, and $2,000 from the sponsoring company, consolidation is not necessary, since the ownership interest of the third party (which is $3,000) is greater than 50 percent of the owner's equity (which is $5,000). But if the SPE's assets are financed with $93,000 in debt, $3,000 from the third party, and $4,000 from the sponsoring company, then consolidation would appear to be necessary because the sponsoring company has the controlling financial interest ($4,000 > $3,000) (See Exhibit 3.13). In Enron's case, the company apparently made an effort to raise at least 3 percent of the SPE's capital from an independent source. However, the 3 percent criterion was not exactly met, and Enron failed to consolidate when it should have. Making matters worse, there was not adequate disclosure that an Enron officer was managing some of the SPEs.

If the sponsoring company is able to structure the SPE to avoid consolidation and even avoid recording a liability for an obligation to the SPE, how does the sponsor manage to receive cash from the SPE and not record the debt? One way is to get the cash by selling assets to the SPE. It is especially helpful to sell some of the sponsor's underperforming assets (like receivables with a high risk of uncollectibility) to the SPE. Financial statement users can be misled when assets appear to be trans-

EXHIBIT 3.13

Examples of Capital Structure for Hypothetical SPEs

SPE 1	Cash and other assets	100,000	
	Bank loans		97,000
	Equity of third party		3,000
SPE 2	Cash and other assets	100,000	
	Bank loans		95,000
	Equity of third party		3,000
	Equity of sponsor		2,000
SPE 3	Cash and other assets	100,000	
	Bank loans		93,000
	Equity of third party		3,000
	Equity of sponsor		4,000

SPE 3 does not qualify to be left off the sponsor's books.

ferred but the risks of ownership of the assets are not transferred to the SPE (as happens when a sponsor promises to buy back the assets in the future).

The lesson in the exposure of apparent extensive use of SPEs in the corporate world is that investors should read the detail in the notes to the financial statements, and if these do not make enough sense, investors should be skeptical.

Summary

One of the basic assumptions underlying financial reporting is that an organization is a going concern. For example, the way certain things are reported, like property, plant and equipment in the balance sheet, depends on assuming that a company has an indefinite life. However, that is not to say that auditors, bankers, credit rating agencies, and others are not on the lookout for possible evidence to the contrary. It is important to be able to identify evidence about a company's liquidity and solvency (or lack thereof). A number of ratios can provide that evidence. In addition, Altman's Z-score can be useful as a red flag.

CHAPTER 4

Analyzing Activity with Financial and Nonfinancial Measures

After reading this chapter, you will be able to

- Evaluate a company's activity level
- Evaluate the separate activity levels of key assets and liabilities
- Measure the productivity of a company's operations
- Compare productivity levels between years or companies
- Understand the concept of capacity usage and how it affects operating leverage
- Calculate operating leverage and total leverage

This chapter discusses techniques used to analyze how effectively and aggressively a company uses its assets. Does it keep its assets active, selling and replacing inventory, and collecting customer accounts receivable? Alternatively, does it allow inventories and receivables to grow old and out of date? Does it use its operating assets productively, or is production uneven and inefficient?

Activity Measures

Turnover ratios are used to measure the activity of a company's assets. The concept of turnover is simple: If a company keeps an inventory of only one unit and sells 100 units during the year, inventory must completely turn over and be replaced 100 times. If, instead, inventory is 100 units, and 100 units are sold, inventory must turn over and be replaced only one time.

At the one-unit inventory level, inventory activity is high. At the 100-unit level, inventory activity is very low. There are advantages and disadvantages to each activity level, high and low. The one-unit inventory (high-activity) level will reduce inventory storage costs but may cause the company top lose sales because the low inventory level does not give customers a selection. Conversely, the 100-unit inventory (low-activity) level will offer a wide selection, but will require higher storage costs and may allow units to become obsolete before they are sold.

We have calculated inventory turnover using units. More frequently, inventory turnover is calculated in dollars. The equation for inventory turnover is

$$\text{Inventory turnover} = \frac{\text{Cost of goods sold}}{\text{Average inventory value}}$$

The general equation for calculating the turnover of an asset is

$$\text{Asset turnover} = \frac{\text{The best measure of asset (or liability) activity}}{\text{Asset (or liability) value}}$$

Each unit that passes through inventory during the year is added to cost of goods sold when it is sold and removed from inventory. This accounting relationship makes cost of goods sold the best measure of activity for the asset inventory. (Still, where cost of goods sold is not readily available in financial statements, some analysts calculate inventory turnover using total sales in the numerator instead of cost of goods sold. This is arguably acceptable where there is a continuing ratio between sales and cost of goods sold and turnover amounts are compared only to other turnover amounts calculated the same way.)

ConAgra Foods is a giant food producer (selling, for instance, 33 million Butterball turkeys last winter). ConAgra's consolidated balance sheet and statement of earnings is shown in Exhibit 4.1.

Using the data from Exhibit 4.1, ConAgra's inventory turnover for the year 2001 is calculated as:

$$\text{Inventory turnover} = \frac{\text{Cost of goods sold}}{\text{Average inventory value}}$$

$$\text{2001 Inventory turnover} = \frac{\$23{,}311{,}700}{\$487{,}700}$$

$$\text{2001 Inventory turnover} = 47.8 \text{ times per year}$$

EXHIBIT 4.1

ConAgra Foods, Inc. and Subsidiaries

Consolidated Statements of Earnings

For the fiscal years ended May	2001	2000	1999
	(in millions except per share amounts)		
Net sales	$ 27,194.2	$ 25,534.6	$ 24,844.4
Costs and expenses			
Cost of goods sold*	23,311.7	22,182.9	21,540.5
Selling, general and administrative expenses*	2,355.1	2,108.1	1,910.9
Interest expense	423.3	303.8	316.6
Restructuring/Impairment charges	—	322.2	440.8
	26,090.1	24,917.0	24,208.8
Income before income taxes and cumulative effect of changes in accounting	1,104.1	617.6	635.6
Income taxes	421.6	235.3	305.4
Income before cumulative effect of changes in accounting	682.5	382.3	330.2
Cumulative effect of changes in accounting	(43.9)	—	—
NET INCOME	$ 638.6	$ 382.3	$ 330.2

EXHIBIT 4.1

CONAGRA FOODS, INC. AND SUBSIDIARIES CONTINUED

For the fiscal years ended May	2001	2000	1999
			(in millions)
INCOME PER SHARE—BASIC			
Income before cumulative effect of changes in accounting	$ 1.33	$ .80	$ .70
Cumulative effect of changes in accounting	(.09)	—	—
NET INCOME	$ 1.24	$ .80	$ .70
INCOME PER SHARE—DILUTED			
Income before cumulative effect of changes in accounting	$ 1.33	$ .80	$ .69
Cumulative effect of changes in accounting	(.09)	—	—
NET INCOME	$ 1.24	$ .80	$ .69

* Other restructuring-related items in fiscal 2000 include accelerated depreciation of $108.3 million and inventory markdowns of $114.5 million included in cost of goods sold and $30.8 million of accelerated depreciation and $45.6 million of restructuring plan implementation costs included in selling, general and administrative expenses.

(The accompanying notes are an integral part of the consolidated financial statements.)

Consolidated Statements of Comprehensive Income

For the fiscal years ended May	2001	2000	1999
			(in millions)
NET INCOME	$ 638.6	$ 382.3	$ 330.2
Other comprehensive income (loss)			
Foreign currency translation adjustment	(17.6)	(37.2)	1.7
COMPREHENSIVE INCOME	$ 621.0	$ 345.1	$ 331.9

(The accompanying notes are an integral part of the consolidated financial statements.)

EXHIBIT 4.1

CONAGRA FOODS, INC. AND SUBSIDIARIES CONTINUED

	May 27 2001	May 28 2000
		(in millions)
ASSETS		
Current assets		
Cash and cash equivalents	$ 198.1	$ 157.6
Receivables, less allowance for doubtful accounts of $100.5 and $62.8	1,605.4	1,241.5
Inventories	5,071.4	4,056.0
Prepaid expenses	487.7	404.8
Total current assets	7,362.6	5,859.9
Property, plant and equipment		
Land	125.4	147.1
Buildings, machinery and equipment	5,776.9	5,430.3
Other fixed assets	640.3	537.0
Construction in progress	308.5	327.4
	6,851.1	6,441.8
Less accumulated depreciation	(2,966.4)	(2,857.8)
Property, plant and equipment, net	3,884.7	3,584.0
Brands, trademarks, and goodwill, at cost less accumulated amortization of $878.7 and $748.3	4,840.2	2,366.0
Other assets	393.3	386.7
	$16,480.8	$12,196.6
LIABILITIES AND STOCKHOLDERS' EQUITY		
Current liabilities		
Notes payable	$ 2,677.1	$1,255.5
Current installments of long-term debt	123.1	20.6
Accounts payable	2,289.8	2,042.5
Advances on sales	349.0	912.7
Accrued payroll	249.7	258.9
Other accrued liabilities	1,246.9	975.2
Total current liabilities	6,935.6	5,465.4

EXHIBIT 4.1

CONAGRA FOODS, INC. AND SUBSIDIARIES CONTINUED

	May 27 2001	May 28 2000
		(in millions)
Senior long-term debt, excluding current installments	3,359.5	1,816.8
Other noncurrent liabilities	927.5	750.7
Subordinated debt	750.0	750.0
Preferred securities of subsidiary company	525.0	525.0
Commitments and contingencies		
Common stockholders' equity		
Common stock of $5 par value, authorized 1,200,000,000 shares; issued 565,337,949 and 524,137,617	2,826.7	2,620.7
Additional paid-in capital	682.5	147.5
Retained earnings	1,534.8	1,345.3
Accumulated other comprehensive income	(120.7)	(103.1)
Less treasury stock, at cost, common shares of 28,270,610 and 31,925,505	(672.9)	(760.2)
	4,250.4	3,250.2
Less unearned restricted stock and value of 12,787,862 and 15,246,068 common shares held in Employee Equity Fund	(267.2)	(361.5)
Total common stockholders' equity	3,983.2	2,888.7
	$16,480.8	$12,196.6

(The accompanying notes are an integral part of the consolidated financial statements.)

Dividing 365 days by inventory turnover provides an estimate of the average number of days a unit remains in inventory. In 2001, ConAgra's units on average remained in inventory for only 7.6 days (365/47.8).

What does this mean? By itself, inventory turnover and the number of days in inventory may mean nothing if not compared to useful standard of some sort. If we calculate ConAgra's inventory turnover and average number of days in inventory for fiscal year 2000, we can detect a pattern.

$$2000\ \text{Inventory turnover} = \frac{\$22{,}182{,}900}{\$404{,}800}$$

2000 Inventory turnover = 54.8 times per year

	2001	**2000**
Inventory turnover (times/year)	47.8	54.8
Number of days in inventory	7.6	6.7

ConAgra's inventory is less active in 2001 than in 2000. It is holding inventory almost a full day longer in 2001 than in 2000. What does this mean? Is the higher inventory level relative to cost of goods sold good or bad? Was ConAgra missing sales because of low inventory levels causing customers to experience poor selection or stockouts? In this case, the change in inventory activity from 2000 to 2001 is good, improving customer selection and preventing stockouts. Was ConAgra unable to generate the inventory sales activity in 2001 as it had in 2000 because of poor performance by the company or the economy?

We might better analyze ConAgra's inventory activity by comparing its activity with the inventory activity of other companies in the same industry or by viewing a longer trend line than the two years given in the financial statements. As it turns out, reading the Letter to Shareholders in ConAgra's annual report provides evidence (see Exhibit 4.2). In the first half of 2001, there were major changes in the economy and in ConAgra's business. ConAgra customers, experiencing the same slowed economic activity, sold less, and as a result, reduced their purchases from ConAgra and cut their own inventory levels.

Turnover of Accounts Receivable

Accounts receivable from customers has a direct link to credit sales as a measure of activity, just as inventory and cost of goods sold were linked.

EXHIBIT 4.2

Excerpt from ConAgra Food 2001 Annual Report Letter to Shareholders

. . . As we started out, the first half of our fiscal year was very promising; but, as we moved into the second half of our fiscal year, which coincided with the start of calendar 2001, we experienced some major shifts in the economy and in our business. Energy costs skyrocketed and the economy slid. Our trade customers got a wake-up call, so they purchased product at a slower rate and made do with less inventory. Our crop inputs distribution business showed weaker orders, declining margins and delinquent accounts. In addition to that, we noticed a few soft spots in other areas, most notably in the retail food sector. As a result, our overall financial performance for fiscal 2001 was not our best. . . .

Sincerely,

Bruce Rohde
Chairman and Chief Executive Officer.

Source: ConAgra Foods Inc., 2001 Annual Report, p. 2.

Every credit sale made increases the amounts in both accounts receivable and sales. When a receivable is collected, the amount of the account receivable is reduced to zero or the actual amount still owed by the customer, but total sales is not reduced. Hence, by the end of the year, sales show the cumulative amount of sales to all customers for the entire year. For a company that sells on credit, total sales is a good measure of how many sales dollars passed through the asset accounts receivable.

The turnover of accounts receivable is calculated as:

$$\text{Accounts receivable turnover} = \frac{\text{Sales}}{\text{Accounts receivable}}$$

IN THE REAL WORLD

The turnover for any asset can be calculated. The accuracy depends on how accurately the numerator value (the "best measure of asset activity") reflects the asset's activity. We could, for instance, calculate the turnover of raw materials in ConAgra's packaged foods segment. We could divide raw materials inventory into the dollar amount of "raw materials used in production." The amounts of raw materials inventory and raw materials used in production are not available in ConAgra's annual report, but the amount would be available to us if we were accountants or managers employed by ConAgra's packaged foods segment.

Using the amounts in Exhibit 4.1, accounts receivable turnover for ConAgra Foods in 2001 is

$$\text{Accounts receivable turnover} = \frac{\$27{,}194{,}200}{\$1{,}605{,}400}$$

$$\text{Accounts receivable turnover} = 16.9 \text{ times per year}$$

Dividing 365 days by accounts receivable turnover provides an estimate of the average number of days required to collect customer accounts receivable. In 2001, ConAgra's collection period for accounts receivable was 21.6 days (365/16.9).

Accounts receivable turnover and the average collection period for 2000 were 20.6 ($25,534,600/$1,241,500) and 17.7 (365/20.6), respectively.

	2001	2000
Accounts receivable turnover (times/year)	16.9	21.6
Average collection period (in days)	20.6	17.7

Why did ConAgra's receivables activity change? The reasons might indicate either good fortune or good management, or just the reverse.

Perhaps ConAgra managers increased the collection period offered in their credit terms, thereby reducing turnover but assisting the sales force in acquiring new customers. Perhaps a recession has forced some ConAgra customers to pay later than usual in order to manage their own cash flow. With only two years' statistics and no data about other companies' receivables, we cannot know why accounts receivable activity slowed, nor whether it signals good or bad.

Again, we are given insight in the Letter to Shareholders, excerpted in Exhibit 4.2, in which the ConAgra chief executive officer (CEO) speaks of the weak market in food products, which leads ConAgra to experience slower payment and uncollectible accounts. In Exhibit 4.1, we see doubtful accounts in 2001 were 60 percent larger in 2001 than in 2000 ($100,500 versus $62,800).

Turnover of Total Assets

Turnover of total assets is a measure of managers' success in keeping the company's total asset base active. The best measure of the activity of total assets is sales. There is no direct link between total assets and sales such as the linkage between inventory and cost of goods sold, or between accounts receivable and sales.

$$\text{Turnover of total assets} = \frac{\text{Sales}}{\text{Total assets}}$$

$$\text{2001 Turnover of total assets} = \frac{\$27,194,200}{\$16,480,800} = 1.65 \text{ times}$$

$$\text{2000 Turnover of total assets} = \frac{\$25,534,600}{\$12,196,600} = 2.1 \text{ times}$$

ConAgra management was less successful in turning over or keeping active the company's assets in 2001 than in 2000. We expected this result because of the decreased turnover of inventory and accounts receivable. (We do not calculate the number of days required to turn over total assets as it has little information value.)

TIPS & TECHNIQUES

The turnover of inventory and accounts receivable examine the activity of two assets often manipulated by managers attempting to bias or fraudulently misstate net income. When the following techniques are used to alter profit, turnover measures are also changed.

For Inventory

Inventory may be increased and expenses reduced by delaying the transfer of inventory cost from the inventory account to cost of goods sold. If $40,000 of inventory is sold in December, but only $30,000 in cost is transferred to cost of goods sold, expenses are $10,000 lower than they should be, profits are $10,000 higher, and inventory turnover is decreased. The company recognizes the sales revenue but not the related cost of goods sold.

Goods placed with merchants on consignment should not be treated as sales until they are, in fact, sold. (A merchant can always return consigned goods that are not sold to the merchant's customers.) If consigned inventory is accounted for as a sale, profit is recorded before it is earned.

For Accounts Receivable

A manager can manipulate reported profits by simply not writing off uncollectible accounts as bad debts expense. If $50,000 in uncollectible accounts is not expensed when the accounts are recognized as uncollectible, reported profit is $50,000 higher than actual profit earned.

Alternatively, a company may increase sales revenue by lowering its standards and granting credit to less creditworthy customers. Sales revenue may then increase but be more than offset by the cost of uncollectible accounts. Accounts receivable would also increase as the customer base expanded, decreasing accounts receivable turnover. However, net accounts receivable (accounts receivable less an allowance for bad debt expense) would then fall because of the higher likelihood of bad debts.

Changes in Productivity

Managers and analysts often cite improvement in a company's productivity as an important benefit arising from new investments or changes in operating processes. Often, increases in productivity are the most important benefit of an investment or process change. This seems true particularly when the investment or process change is technology related. However, most productivity improvements in such assertions are often never quantified. There may be a total dollar benefit to compare with a proposed or actual cost, but the portion of the benefit resulting from a productivity change is not calculated. This may be true because determining dollar benefit accompanying a change in productivity is not straightforward.

Productivity is measured as output per unit of input.

Productivity rate = output / input

One difficulty in measuring productivity in some organizations is in determining what *output* is. For a police force, is output measured by the number of speeders ticketed? Alternatively, by the absence of speeders? If the goal is to stop motorists from speeding, how do you measure the absence of speeders as an output? The problem measuring output is greater in governmental and not-for-profit organizations. Most for-profit entities can clearly identify their output.

Comparing Years

Stillwater Mining Company has a clearly identifiable and easily measured output. Stillwater mines and mills (extracts) palladium and platinum in Montana. In its 2000 annual report, Stillwater reported operating data for several years. An excerpt from Selected Financial and Operating Data in Stillwater's Financial Review, reproduced in Exhibit 4.3, shows that Stillwater produced 409,000 ounces of palladium and platinum (com-

EXHIBIT 4.3

Stillwater Mining Company: Excerpt from 2000 Annual Report

Financial Review—Selected Financial and Operating Data

	2000	1999	1998	1997	1996
	(in thousands, except per share amounts)				
Operating Data					
Tons milled[5]	756	689	719	577	446
Mill head grade[6]	0.64	0.66	0.69	0.70	0.67
Ounces of palladium produced	330	315	340	271	196
Ounces of platinum produced	100	94	104	84	59
Total ounces produced[7]	430	409	444	355	255
Ounces of palladium sold	324	314	337	288	214
Ounces of platinum sold	100	94	103	91	62
Total ounces sold[7]	424	408	440	379	276
Price and Cost Data[8]					
Average realized price per palladium ounce	$ 560	$ 372	$ 202	$ 144	$ 144
Average realized price per platinum ounce	481	383	377	388	410
Combined average realized price per ounce	541	375	243	203	204
Average market price per palladium ounce	$ 680	$ 358	$ 286	$ 178	$ 128
Average market price per platinum ounce	544	377	372	395	397
Combined average market price per ounce	649	362	304	230	191

EXHIBIT 4.3

STILLWATER MINING COMPANY: EXCERPT FROM 2000 ANNUAL REPORT CONTINUED

	2000	1999	1998	1997	1996
	(in thousands, except per share amounts)				
Total cash costs per ton milled	$ 150	$ 117	$ 93	$ 107	$ 105
Total cash costs per ounce produced	264	198	151	174	184
Total production costs per ounce produced	305	231	178	207	219

(5) Tons milled represent the number of grade-bearing tons of ore and sub-grade material fed to the concentrator.

(6) Milled head grade is presented as ounces of palladium and platinum combined per ton.

(7) Ounces produced is defined as the number of ounces shipped from the concentrator during the period reduced by losses expected to be incurred in subsequent smelting and refining processes. Differences in ounces produced and ounces sold are caused by the length of time required by the smelting and refining processes.

(8) A combined average realized price and market price of palladium and platinum are reported at the same ratio as ounces are produced from the base metals refinery. Total cash costs include costs of mining, processing and administrative expenses at the mine site (including overhead, taxes other than income taxes, royalties and credits for metals produced other than palladium and platinum). Total production costs include total cash costs plus depreciation and amortization. Income taxes, corporate general and administrative expenses and interest income and expense are not included in either total cash costs or total production costs.

Source: Stillwater Mining Company, 2000 Annual Report, p. 37.

bined) from 689,000 tons of ore mined in fiscal year 1999. The same figures for 2000 are 430,000 ounces of palladium and platinum from 756,000 tons of ore. Productivity rate calculations for 1999 and 2000 follow.

$$1999\ \text{Productivity rate} = \frac{1999\ \text{Ounces of palladium and platinum}}{1999\ \text{Tons of ore}}$$

1999 Productivity rate = 409,000 oz/689,000 tons

1999 Productivity rate = .593 oz/ton

$$2000\ \text{Productivity rate} = \frac{2000\ \text{Ounces of palladium and platinum}}{2000\ \text{Tons of ore}}$$

2000 Productivity rate = 430,000 oz/756,000 tons

2000 Productivity rate = .568 oz/ton

In Stillwater's productivity decreased from 1999 to 2000. The problem is quantifying the change. Productivity changed by .025 ounces (.593 – .568) per ton. By what total amount in tons or dollars year to year? To determine a total change, we must restate the productivity equation so that we solve for inputs rather than the rate.

Productivity rate = Output/Input
(Productivity rate)(inputs) = Output
Inputs = Output/Productivity rate

Now we can compare the inputs that would be required in 2000 if productivity had remained at the higher 1999 rate.

Inputs required = 2000 Output / 1999 Productivity rate

Inputs required = 430,000 oz / .593 oz/ton

Inputs required = 725,126 tons

Thus, theoretically, 725,126 tons would have been required in 2000 if the mines had operated at the 1999 productivity level. What does that mean?

Theoretical inputs at 1999 productivity rate	725,126 tons
Actual inputs at 2000 productivity rate	756,000 tons
Difference	30,874 tons

Because productivity decreased during the year, the year 2000 required 756,000 tons of ore milled, rather than the 725,126 that would have been required using the 1999 productivity rate.

Elsewhere in its annual report, Stillwater says: "In 2001 the mine is expected to produce 500,000 ounces of palladium and platinum from milling ore at an average rate of 2,300 tons per day." This tells us Stillwater forecasts output of 500,000 ounces from an input of 839,500 total tons milled (2,300 tons/day × 365 days), or a production rate of .596 ounces/ton (500,000 oz / 839,500 tons) in 2001, approximately equal to the 1999 rate.

Exhibit 4.3 also tells us the "total cash costs per ton milled" enabling us to calculate productivity rates and changes in dollars.

Productivity rate calculations in dollars for 1999 and 2000 follow.

$$\text{1999 Productivity rate (in dollars)} = \frac{\text{1999 Ounces of palladium and platinum}}{\text{(1999 tons)} \times \text{(1999 \$/ton)}}$$

1999 Productivity rate = 409,000 oz/(689,000 tons) × ($117,000/ton)

1999 Productivity rate = .0000049 oz/dollar cash cost

$$\text{2000 Productivity rate (in dollars)} = \frac{\text{2000 Ounces of palladium and platinum}}{\text{(2000 tons)} \times \text{(2000 \$/ton)}}$$

2000 Productivity rate = 430,000 oz/(756,000 tons) × ($150,000)

2000 Productivity rate = .0000037 oz/dollar cash cost

The oz/dollar cash cost can also be determined as the reciprocal of the "Total cash cost per ounce produced," shown in the excerpt from Stillwater's Financial Review, in Exhibit 4.3. For 1999, total cash cost per unit produced is, in dollars per ounce, $117,000; thus, the reciprocal in ounces per dollar is .000005 oz/dollar, as calculated here. For 2000, Total cash cost per unit produced is, in dollars per ounce, $150,000; the reciprocal in ounces per dollar is .000005 oz/dollar, also calculated here.

We can also compare productivity measured in dollars during 1999 and 2000 using the equation from before. We can compare the inputs in dollars that would have been required in 2000 if productivity had remained at the 1999 rate and isolate the dollar benefit or penalty of the change.

Inputs = Output/Productivity rate

Inputs required = 2000 Output / 1999 Productivity rate

Inputs required = 430,000 oz/ .0000049 oz/dollar

Inputs required = $877,551 (in millions)

Thus, theoretically, $877,551 (in millions) would have been required in 2000 if the mines had operated at the 1999 productivity level. What does that mean?

	(in millions)
Theoretical inputs at 1999 productivity rate	$877,551
Actual inputs at 2000 productivity rate	113,400
(756,000 tons milled × $150,000/ton)	
Difference	$746,600

Because productivity decreased during the year, the year 2000 required 756,000 tons of ore milled, rather than the 725,126 that would have been required using the 1999 productivity rate.

Capacity Usage

In addition to keeping assets active and productive, managers seek to use all available operating capacity. It is costly for a company to own and pay for unused capacity. The cost of unused capacity is frequently calculated as a production variance, although unlike production variances such as a labor efficiency variance, or raw material usage variances, there is not much a production manager can do to increase production and reduce the capacity usage variance. Sales must obtain orders from customers that in turn cause increases in production. Additional production in the absence of additional sales is dysfunctional.

Most of a company's capacity costs are committed fixed costs—committed in that management must incur the costs to maintain the capability to operate. The costs are called fixed because changes in operating activity do not generally cause changes in total capacity cost. Capacity costs are composed of charges such as such as lease payments on equipment, supervisory salaries, insurance, property taxes, and so forth.

Exhibit 4.4 contains a graph of the committed, fixed cost of an equipment lease over a range of activity for a small factory. The lease cost is a capacity cost, necessary for production to take place, and not subject to change when production activity changes within the company's normal range.

Operating costs, other than capacity costs, are largely variable costs that are not always necessary to maintaining the capacity to produce, and do change in total when total production activity changes. Examples of

EXHIBIT 4.4

Capacity Cost
Graph of a Fixed Cost: Equipment Lease Versus Production Activity

Activity is measured by the number of units produced.

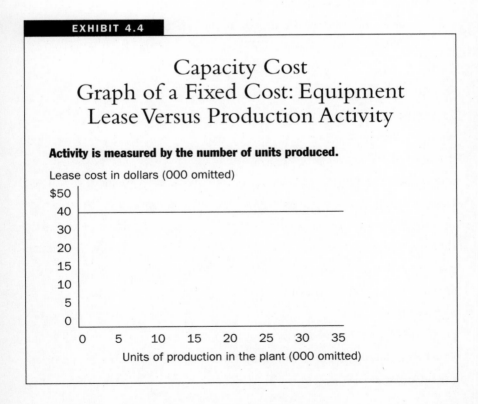

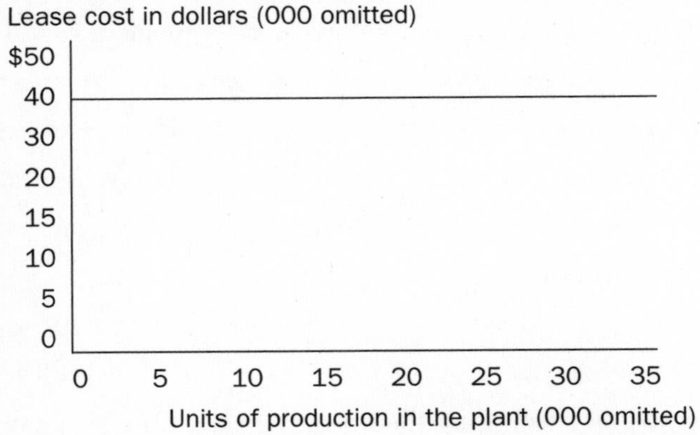

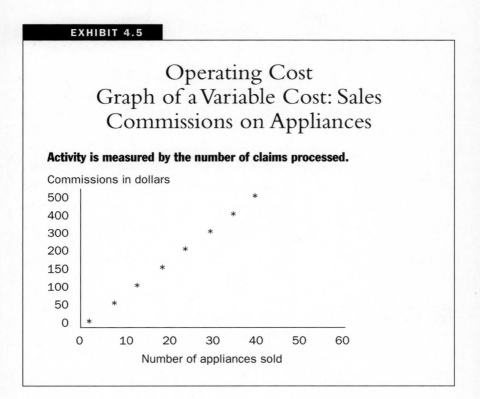

EXHIBIT 4.5

Operating Cost Graph of a Variable Cost: Sales Commissions on Appliances

Activity is measured by the number of claims processed.

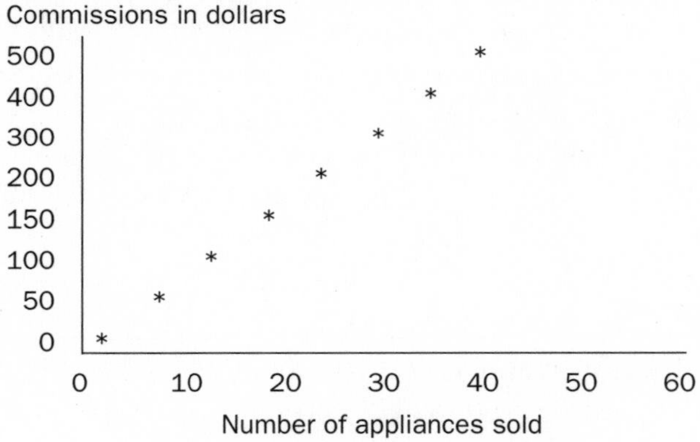

variable operating costs include raw materials used, plant labor, sales commissions, supplies, and energy. Exhibit 4.5 is a graph of supplies used in an insurance claims office.

Often, there is a trade-off between variable operating costs and fixed capacity costs. For example, let us examine Acme Inc., a hypothetical company. If Acme has a manual process that costs $50 per unit to perform. If this process is automated, the cost per unit of the process may perhaps be reduced to $40 per unit. The automation may require the purchase of a $50,000 machine, raising capacity costs from $100,000 to $150,000. If the product sells for $60 per unit, profit for the manual and the automated operations at the same 10,000-unit level of sales is:

Acme, Inc. **Before Automation**	**Total**		**Per Unit**
Sales (10,000 units × $60/unit)	$600,000	$60	100.0%
Variable costs (10,000 units × $40/unit)	400,000	40	66.7
Contribution margin	200,000	$20	33.3%
Fixed capacity costs	100,000		
Profit	$100,000		

Acme, Inc. **After Automation**			
Sales (10,000 units × $60/unit)	$600,000	$60	100.0%
Variable costs (10,000 units × $30/unit)	300,000	30	50.0
Contribution margin	300,000	$20	50.0%
Fixed capacity costs	150,000		
Profit	$150,000		

Balancing the relative components of variable and fixed cost to generate an increase in profit is called maximizing *operating leverage*. The mix of variable and fixed costs before automation yields only $20/unit contribution to cover fixed costs and build profit, compared to $30/unit with the cost mix after the process is automated.

The increase in contribution margin/unit causes an increase in sales to have a bigger impact on profit. If sales increase 1,000 units, profits are increased only $20,000 ($20/unit × 1,000 units) before automation, but after automation a 1,000 unit increase in sales increases profits by $30,000 ($30/unit × 1,000 units). The increase in contribution margin brought about by the new cost mix leverages the impact of a change in sales on profit.

There is, however, a downside to leverage. Not only does an increase in sales yield a larger increase in profit, a decrease in sales also yields a larger decrease in profit. In other words, the behavior of profit is more volatile when operating leverage is high. The mix of fixed and variable costs after automation leverages, or magnifies, the effect of any change in sales.

Calculating Operating Leverage

A company's operating leverage is measured at a particular proportion of fixed and variable costs. Operating leverage is the percentage change in operating earnings (i.e., earnings before interest and taxes and any non-operating income) that accompanies a percentage change in contribution margin, when in sales volume is changed. As we notice below, the percentage change in sales is the same as the percentage change in contribution margin. To illustrate, we calculate Acme's operating leverage with the automated process at both 10,000 units sales (as above) and increased to 12,000 units (as follows).

Acme, Inc.
After automation-sales increased to 12,000 units

Sales (12,000 units × $60/unit)	$720,000	$60	100.0%
Variable costs (12,000 units × $30/unit)	360,000	30	50.0
Contribution margin	360,000	$30	50.0%
Fixed capacity costs	150,000		
Profit	$210,000		

	Base	**Increased**	**% Change**
Sales in units	10,000	12,000	20%
Sales in dollars	$600,000	$720,000	20%
Contribution margin	$300,000	$360,000	20%
Operating income	$150,000	$210,000	40%

$$\text{Degree of operating leverage} = \frac{\%\ \text{Change in operating income}}{\%\ \text{Change in sales}}$$

Degree of operating leverage = 40%/20% = 2

This means that a certain percentage change in sales will result in two times as large a percentage change in operating earnings. So, if sales increase another 1,000 units (a 3,000/10,000 = .30 increase), operating earnings will increase by [.30 × 2]= 60%. The $150,000 operating income increases by [.60 × $150,000] = $90,000, or $240,000 in total.

Acme, Inc. **After automation-sales increased to 13,000 units**			
Sales (13,000 units × $60/unit)	$780,000	$60	100.0%
Variable costs (13,000 units × $30/unit)	390,000	30	50.0
Contribution margin	390,000	$30	50.0%
Fixed capacity costs	150,000		
Profit	$240,000		

	Base	**Increased**	**$ Change**
Sales in units	10,000	13,000	—
Sales in dollars	$600,000	$780,000	$180,000
Contribution margin	$300,000	$390,000	$ 90,000
Operating income	$150,000	$240,000	$ 90,000

The same calculation result can be achieved from the financial statements for a single year (a single activity level) using the following formula:

$$\text{Degree of operating leverage} = \frac{\text{Contribution margin}}{\text{Operating income}}$$

At 10,000 units of sales and assuming the cost structure and operating leverage is as above, the degree of operating leverage is

$$\text{Degree of operating leverage} = \frac{\$300,000}{\$150,000} = 2$$

The equation is useful because it lets us calculate the degree of operating leverage in a company's cost structure from one year of its earnings. Still, its usefulness is limited to companies examining their own operations as published financial statements do not show cost separated by behavior (and hence do not show contribution margin) in either the income statement or the balance sheet.

If we wish to calculate the degree of operating leverage of ConAgra, used earlier in the chapter, we must use two years' data because contribution margin is not shown. We must use change in sales rather than the contribution margin. ConAgra's degree of operating leverage is 1.2, calculated below.

	2001	2000	% Change
Sales in dollars	$27,194.2	$25,534.6	6.5
Operating income	$ 1,104.1	$ 617.6	7.9

$$\text{Degree of operating leverage} = \frac{\text{\% Change in operating income}}{\text{\% Change in sales}}$$

$$\text{Degree of operating leverage} = 1.2$$

Measuring Total Leverage

ConAgra levers its operations to produce increased operating income by adjusting its mix of fixed and variable costs. It also levers its operating income to yield increased earnings by adjusting the debt to equity mix in its capital structure. Operating leverage is sometimes called first-stage leverage, and financial leverage is sometimes called second-stage leverage. Financial leverage is discussed in Chapter 3.

Sales	
Operating expenses	First-stage, operating leverage
Operating earnings	
Interest and taxes	Second-stage, financial leverage
Net income	

ConAgra's total leverage is the product of its financial and operating leverage. The formula for calculating total leverage follows.

$$\text{Degree of total leverage} = \frac{\text{\% Change in [operating income} - \text{interest]}}{\text{\% Change in sales}}$$

For ConAgra:

$$\text{Degree of total leverage} = \frac{1.169}{.065}$$

Summary

This chapter examined the effectiveness and efficiency of a company's operating activity. An effective company has an appropriately high level of activity. An efficient company has a high level of productivity, a high level of capacity usage and uses operating leverage to increase profit. While maximizing of these factors requires balancing risk and security, measuring and benchmarking a company's current pattern of operations is the correct place to begin.

CHAPTER 5

Quality of Earnings and Cash Flows

After reading this chapter, you will be able to

- Understand issues involving quality of earnings
- Calculate ratios based on various types of cash flows
- Understand the use of common-size cash flow statements
- Understand the use of common-size income statements and balance sheets

A lot has been made lately about "opaqueness versus transparency" in financial reporting and an "aggressive" approach to accounting. These issues reflect a concern with obtaining information that is useful because it reflects the true financial condition of a company. After the country was caught off guard in the Enron disaster, there was much questioning about why information was not available about, for example, the amount of debt and risk the company had, the drag on earnings that poorly performing assets caused, the presence of related-party situations that were not adequately disclosed—the list could go on. Many stakeholders needed to know about these things. Many stakeholders now are pushing for improvements in the quality of financial reporting, including the quality of earnings.

The conventional wisdom is that information about historical net income is more predictive of future cash flows than are historical cash flows. Proponents of accrual net income can point out that the timing of cash flows can be manipulated. But proponents of cash flow information can point out that the amount of judgment involved in calculating net income can lead to manipulation of net income, or, in a better light, the management of net income. It is not unheard of that some companies "help" analysts predict earnings so that the company can hit the target earnings per share (EPS); there is pressure for a company to at least meet its target EPS because falling short of it can adversely affect the company's stock price.

Quality of Earnings

In the long run, net income should be about equal to cash flows because a company is normally in business in order to earn cash. The timing may be slightly different. That is, a company may get cash and subsequently do something to earn it or the company may earn revenues by delivering services or products and then later receive the cash. The closer the amount of net earnings is to the amount of cash flow in the short run, the higher the perception of the quality of earnings.

Another issue is the sustainability of earnings. Earnings are higher quality if they will be ongoing rather than just a blip on the screen. For example, a company may convince customers at year end to go on and stock up on their product. There may also be included the implied promise or assumption that the company will buy back the product some time after year end if necessary. The result is a surge in sales at year end that will likely not be repeated for quite a while. So earnings in the current year may be greater than earnings in the following year.

The timing of expense recognition is also a way to increase earnings in the current year. For instance, managers could delay necessary maintenance from December to January in order to avoid the negative impact on earnings.

In addition to managing the timing of revenues and expenses, companies can engage in questionable transactions or poor business practices to boost revenues. Managers may extend credit to poor credit risks in order to boost sales; or they may postpone the write-down of obsolete inventory in order to avoid the charge against earnings; or they may engage in swaps of a product or service in order to increase revenue from sale of a product to another company and increase assets from purchase of the same product from the other party.

Differences between Net Income and Cash Flows

The cash flow statement has three main sections, the first of which is *cash from operations*. Most companies use the indirect method, which involves starting with net income and making adjustments to net income to arrive at cash from operations. Those adjustments are mainly the addition of noncash expenses (like depreciation and amortization), the subtraction of noncash gains, and additions or subtractions of changes in current accounts.

Net income	$10,000
+ Depreciation and amortization	2,000
– Increases in accounts receivable	(500)
+ Decreases in inventory	600
+ Increases in accounts payable	300
– Decreases in wages payable	(200)
= Cash from operations	$12,200

So the nice thing is that all the information is in the same place, and one can see at a glance why cash from operations is different from net income. In the above example, depreciation and amortization are the single biggest reason that the income and cash flow differ. For some companies it is apparent when depreciation is the main reason that cash from operations is positive but net income negative (i.e., a net loss). For example, in the above calculation, if there had been a net loss of $1,500, the cash from operations would be $700.

Depreciation and amortization, therefore, present a very obvious area in which to manage earnings since there are estimates needed and choices available.

Accounting Methods and Perceived Quality of Earnings

Companies choose among alternative accounting methods. When a company chooses an accounting method because it maximizes reported earnings, investors view the resulting reported earnings as lower quality. Studies have shown, for instance, that investors see a company that chooses to use straight-line depreciation as having lower-quality earnings than a company that uses an accelerated method.[1]

Exhibit 5.1 shows the difference between straight-line and accelerated sum-of-the-years'-digits (SYD) depreciation for a $2,000 machine with a four-year life and no salvage value. SYD depreciation yields higher depreciation expense and lower net income than straight-line in the first two years of the machine's life, but the situation is exactly reversed in the last two years. Over the machine's four-year life, both methods result in the same total depreciation expense and earnings.

Also, regardless of the depreciation method used for financial reporting, a company is free for tax reporting to use the depreciation method that results in the lowest tax liability—so the choice of depreciation method for earnings does not result in different cash flows, only in different reported earnings.

In theory, investors (as a group) "see" the company's real earnings, regardless of the accounting method used, as long as appropriate disclosures are made. Thus, the higher earnings brought about solely by accounting treatment are "seen" as lower quality.

EXHIBIT 5.1

Straight-Line and Accelerated Depreciation Expense

Year	Straight-line Depreciation (1)	Sum-of-the-years'-digits Depreciation (2)	Difference (2) – (1)
1	$ 500	$ 800	$ 300
2	500	600	100
3	500	400	(100)
4	500	200	(300)
Total	$2,000	$2,000	$ 0

This exhibit shows the difference between straight-line and the accelerated sum-of-the-years'-digits depreciation for a $2,000 machine with a four-year life.

Accounting Methods that Change Cash Flows

When companies choose between accounting methods, some choices affect cash flows because the same accounting method must be used for both financial reporting and tax reporting. Inventory methods fall into this group; a company must use the same inventory method for both financial and tax reporting. Last-in, first-out (LIFO) and first-in, first-out (FIFO) affect both reported earnings and cash flows for taxes. These two methods are used to illustrate the effect of such accounting methods on the quality of earnings.

Assume in a period of rising prices, a company has beginning inventory of one unit costing $15 and purchases two more units for $18 each.

Beginning inventory	1 unit @ $15/unit	$15
Purchase	2 units @ $18/unit	36
Total available for sale	3 units	$51

If the company sells one unit for $30, LIFO and FIFO inventory methods result in gross profit and ending inventory amounts as follows:

	LIFO	FIFO
In the income statement:		
Sales	$30	$30
Cost of goods sold	18	15
Gross profit	12	15
In the balance sheet:		
Inventory	33	36
	(15 + 18)	(18 + 18)

When a company uses FIFO inventory during a period of rising inventory replacement costs, the company charges the cost of older, lower cost inventory to cost of goods sold: here, $15. This results in a cost of goods sold expense that is less than the cash required to replace the inventory sold. In our example, $18 is the cost of units most recently purchased. To replace the unit sold, the company can be expected to spend $18 cash or more. If the company must spend $18 (or more) to replace the unit sold, operating cash flows using FIFO are

Cash inflow from sales	$30
Cash outflow to replace the unit sold	18
Net cash inflow from operations	$12
Reported gross profit	15
Excess gross profit over cash inflow	$ 3

Reported earnings are greater than the increase in real net assets (cash from operations), and this reduces the quality of reported earnings.

If, instead, the company uses LIFO inventory, the $18 cost of the most recent inventory purchased is charged to cost of goods sold. If the company must spend $18 (or more) to replace the unit sold, operating cash flows using LIFO are

Cash inflow from sales	$30
Cash outflow to replace the unit sold	18
Net cash inflow from operations	$12
Reported gross profit	12
Excess gross profit over cash inflow	$ 0

This cost of goods sold expense is much closer to the amount of cash required to replace the inventory sold and reported earnings are closer to cash from operations.

Thus, it would appear that earnings are of higher quality when companies use LIFO rather than FIFO. This is true when prices are rising or falling: The most current prices expensed using LIFO are always closer to replacement cost than the older costs expensed under FIFO.

The Effect of Taxes

In addition to the effect on the difference between reported earnings and cash flows, the choice in inventory methods also affects taxes paid, because a company must use the same method for filing taxes that was used to report income to shareholders. When prices are rising, companies that use FIFO pay more income tax than companies that use LIFO.

Assume in the example above that the company had $6 in other expenses and the tax rate was 35 percent.

	LIFO	FIFO
Sales	$30	$30
Cost of goods sold	18	15
Gross profit	12	15
Other expenses	6	6
Net income before tax	6	9
Income tax	2.1	3.2
Net income	$ 3.9	$ 5.8

The company pays higher taxes using FIFO than LIFO. If prices were falling instead of rising, the reverse would be true; the most current prices (charged to cost of goods sold under LIFO) would be the lowest, and LIFO would result in the highest income and the highest income tax paid.

LIFO Reserve in the Financial Statements

The Internal Revenue Service (IRS) will allow companies to use LIFO for tax reporting only if they also use it for financial reporting. These companies can, however, report an alternative inventory amount (usually FIFO) in the notes to the financial statements or through the use of a LIFO reserve. (A company does not have the same requirement regarding FIFO or weighted average. A company could use weighted average for taxes and FIFO for financial reporting, for example.)

A LIFO reserve is the difference between LIFO cost and the replacement cost of the inventory (usually assumed to be FIFO cost). This difference occurs because LIFO shows inventories at older, often lower costs than if the inventories were shown at their (FIFO) replacement cost. If, for example, LIFO inventory is $40, and FIFO inventory is $50, the LIFO reserve is $10, the difference between the two. Some companies show the LIFO reserve on the balance sheet, some in the notes.

When the LIFO reserve is shown, statement readers know the current replacement cost of the inventories and the company receives the tax and other benefits of using LIFO. The LIFO reserve allows readers to compare companies using LIFO with companies using FIFO. Because a LIFO reserve is the difference between LIFO cost and the replacement cost of the inventory (usually assumed to be FIFO cost), we can use the LIFO reserve to determine the effect of the LIFO/FIFO choice on the quality of earnings. For example, Exhibit 5.2 shows Dow Chemical's footnote disclosure of its LIFO reserve.

EXHIBIT 5.2

Dow Chemical's Note E on Inventories

Note E: Inventories

The reserves required to adjust inventories from the first-in, first-out ("FIFO") basis to the last-in, first-out ("LIFO") basis amounted to a decrease of $146 at December 31, 2001, and a decrease of $682 at December 31, 2000. The inventories that were valued on a LIFO basis, principally hydrocarbon and U.S. chemicals and plastics product inventories, represented 36 percent of the total inventories at December 31, 2001, and 38 percent of the total inventories at December 31, 2000.

A reduction of certain inventories resulted in the liquidation of some quantities of LIFO inventory, which increased pre-tax income $19 in 2001, $67 in 2000, and $51 in 1999.

Source: The Dow Chemical Company 2001 annual report, p. 52.

The Use of Cash Flow Information in Ratio Analysis

So many ratios are based on the balance sheet only (leverage ratios) or the income statement only (e.g., margin ratios) or on accounts from both income statement and balance sheet (e.g., turnover ratios). Sometimes, doubts about the quality of earnings lead to more of a focus on cash flows. Ratios based on information from the cash flow statement can be useful to add to the information gained from analysis of traditional ratios. It is often cash flow problems that can push a company into bankruptcy; for example, look what happened to Kmart when it could not make a payment to one of its food suppliers.

Mills and Yamamura[2] discuss two main categories of cash flow ratios, with each with a different focus. Some of these are discussed briefly in Chapter 2 and are repeated here for comparative purposes:

1. Liquidity and solvency
- Operating cash flow (OCF)
- Funds flow coverage (FFC)
- Cash interest coverage (CIC)
- Cash debt coverage (CDC)

2. Going concern
- Cash to capital expenditures (C/CE)
- Cash to total debt (C/TD)
- Total free cash (TFC)
- Cash flow adequacy (CFA)

Operating Cash Flow Ratio

The operating cash flow ratio is closest to (or most similar to) the current ratio (i.e., current assets/current liabilities). As such, it shows the company's ability to generate cash from its operations, to cover its current liabilities.

$$\text{Operating cash flow} = \frac{\text{Cash flow from operations}}{\text{Current liabilities}}$$

The numerator comes straight from the cash flow statement. It is the subtotal of the operating section (the first one) and is the result of starting with net income and making certain adjustments for noncash expenses and revenues, and for changes in current assets and current liabilities. Exhibit 5.3 shows the OCF for 2001 and 2000 for Pfizer. The company's OCF in 2000 was \$.52 in cash from operations for every \$1.00 in current liabilities, which seems like a tenuous situation to be in. However, it increases to \$.68 in 2001.

EXHIBIT 5.3

Pfizer Inc. Cash Flow Analysis

Liquidity	2001	2000
1. Operating cash flow OCF	$= \frac{\$9,291}{13,640} = 0.68$	$\frac{\$6,195}{11,981} = 0.52$
2. Funds flow coverage FFC*	$= \frac{\$32,259 - 5,034 - 11,299 + 1,068 - 4,847}{\$303 + (151/.745) + 0}$	$\frac{\$29,355 - 5,007 - 11,223 + 968 - 4,435}{\$460 + (529/.728) + 0}$
	$= \frac{\$12,147}{\$506} = 24.01$	$= \frac{\$9,658}{\$1,187} = 8.14$
3. Cash interest coverage CIC	$= \frac{\$9,291 + \$303 + \$1,006}{\$303} = 34.98$	$\frac{\$6,195 + \$460 + \$1,041}{\$460} = 16.73$
4. Cash current debt coverage CDC	$= \frac{\$9,291 - \$2,715}{\$6,265} = 1.05$	$\frac{\$6,195 - \$2,197}{\$4,289} = 0.93$

* Using effective tax rates of 25.5% and 27.2%.

EXHIBIT 5.3

Pfizer Inc. Cash Flow Analysis

Going Concern	2001	2000
5. Cash to capital expenditures C/CE	$= \frac{\$9,291}{\$2,203} = 4.22$	$\frac{\$6,195}{\$2,191} = 2.83$
6. Cash to total debt C/TD	$= \frac{\$9,291}{\$20,860} = 0.45$	$\frac{\$6,195}{\$17,434} = 0.36$
7. Total free cash flow TFC	$= \frac{\$4,406}{\$7,032} = 0.63$	$\frac{\$684}{\$5,339} = 0.13$
8. Cash flow adequacy (CFA) (using the numerator from the funds flow coverage)	$= \frac{\$12,147 - 1,006 - 303 - 2,203}{\$552}$	$\frac{\$9,658 - 1,041 - 460 - 2,191}{\$445}$
	$= \frac{\$8,635}{\$522} = 16.54$	$\frac{\$5,966}{\$445} = 13.41$

To calculate EBITDA, we subtracted the first three expenses from sales and added back depreciation and amortization from the cash flow statement.

To adjust for taxes, we divided by 1 – tax rate. In the calculation above, we used the effective tax rates disclosed in Pfizer's annual report.

Funds Flow Coverage Ratio

The funds flow coverage ratio is based on earnings before interest, taxes, depreciation, and amortization (EBITDA), which is often heralded as being a number fairly close to cash from operations.

$$\text{Funds flow coverage} = \frac{\text{EBITDA}}{\text{Interest} + \text{Tax-adjusted debt payment} + \text{Tax-adjusted preferred dividends}}$$

The results shown in Exhibit 5.3 demonstrate the ability to cover unavoidable expenditures like interest, debt, and preferred dividends (for Pfizer there were none). Pfizer's coverage improved almost 200 percent from 2000 to 2001.

Cash Interest Coverage Ratio

The cash interest coverage ratio conveys the company's ability to pay the interest on its debt. The numerator therefore measures the cash before interest and tax payments are made.

$$\text{Cash interest coverage} = \frac{\text{Cash flow from operations} + \text{Interest paid} + \text{Taxes paid}}{\text{Interest paid}}$$

This ratio is comparable to the traditional TIE ratio (times interest earned), but could be said to be more useful since interest payments have to be met with cash, not accrual basis earnings. Pfizer's coverage more than doubled.

Cash Current Debt Coverage Ratio

The cash current debt coverage ratio highlights the company's ability to still pay its debt after it distributes dividends.

$$\text{Cash current debt coverage} = \frac{\text{Operating cash flow} - \text{Cash dividends}}{\text{Current debt}}$$

Current debt is not necessarily all current liabilities, but rather debt maturing within one year. Generally, a coverage ratio should be at least one. Pfizer's coverage went from less than one to more than one in 2001.

Cash to Capital Expenditures Ratio

The cash to capital expenditures ratio looks at a bigger picture than do the previous four ratios, because they reflect liquidity, whereas cash to capital expenditures focuses on company health and growth.

$$\text{Cash to capital expenditure} = \frac{\text{Cash flow from operations}}{\text{Capital expenditures}}$$

This ratio indicates whether a company can take advantage of opportunities for growth and still pay off debt. This measure also shows improvement for Pfizer.

Cash to Total Debt Ratio

The usefulness of this ratio is fairly obvious.

$$\text{Cash to total debt} = \frac{\text{Cash flow from operations}}{\text{Total debt}}$$

Of course, the higher the better since it measures a company's ability to pay off its liabilities. For Pfizer, the cash to total debt improved.

Total Free Cash Flow Ratio

This total free cash flow ratio defines free cash flow slightly differently from the previous definition (in Chapter 2) which points up the fact that there is no standard definition of free cash flow.

$$\text{Total free cash flow} = \frac{\text{Net income} + \text{Accrued and capitalized interest expense} + \text{Depreciation and amortization} + \text{Operating lease and rental expense} - \text{Declared dividends} - \text{Capital expenditures}}{\text{Accrued and capitalized interest expense} + \text{Operating lease and rental expense} + \text{Current portion of long-term debt} + \text{Current portion of capitalized lease obligations}}$$

Such a ratio might send one on a wild goose chase through the numbers in an annual report. Depending on how a company classifies balances in its financial statements and discloses detail in its notes, it may be necessary to modify the above ratio somewhat. For Pfizer (whose income statement is shown in Exhibit 5.4), the information is found as follows:

	2001	2000	Source
The Numerator:			
Net income	$7,788	$3,726	Income statement
+ Accrued and capitalized interest	322	432	Note 10: Other income
+ Depreciation and amortization	1,068	968	Cash flow statement
+ Operating lease and rental expense	300	318	Note 13: Lease commitments
– Declared dividends	(2,869)	(2,569)	Consolidated Statements of Shareholders' Equity
– Capital expenditures	(2,203)	(2,191)	Cash flow statement
Numerator	$4,406	$ 684	
The Denominator:			
Accrued and capitalized interest	$322	$432	See above
+ Operating lease and rental expense	300	318	See above
+ Current portion of long-term debt	6,265	4,289	Consolidated balance sheet
+ Current portion of capitalized lease obligations	145	300	Note 13: Lease commitments
Denominator	$7,032	$5,339	

It looks as if Pfizer has improved in its ability to meet future cash commitments. But still, the company, after paying dividends and acquiring plant assets, does not have enough to cover basic commitments for fixed expenditures like interest and debt. This would not be a viable situation in the long run without having to obtain additional financing.

EXHIBIT 5.4

Pfizer Inc. and Subsidiary Companies

Consolidated Statement of Income

	Year ended December 31		
	2001	**2000**	**1999**
	(in millions, except per share data)		
Revenues	$ 32,259	$ 29,355	$ 27,166
Costs and expenses:			
Cost of sales	5,034	5,007	5,576
Selling, informational and administrative expenses	11,299	11,223	10,600
Research and development expenses	4,847	4,435	4,036
Merger-related costs	839	3,257	33
Other income— net	(89)	(348)	(24)
Income from continuing operations before provision for taxes on income and minority interests	10,329	5,781	6,945
Provision for taxes on income	2,561	2,049	1,968
Minority interests	16	14	5
Income from continuing operations	7,752	3,718	4,972
Discontinued operations—net of tax	36	8	(20)
Net income	$ 7,788	$ 3,726	$ 4,952
EARNINGS PER COMMON SHARE—BASIC			
Income from continuing operations	$ 1.25	$ .60	$ .81
Discontinued operations—net of tax	—	—	—
Net income	$ 1.25	$ .60	$ .81
EARNINGS PER COMMON SHARE—DILUTED			
Income from continuing operations	$ 1.22	$ .59	$ .79
Discontinued operations—net of tax	—	—	(.01)
Net income	$ 1.22	$ .59	$ .78
Weighted average shares—basic	6,239	6,210	6,126
Weighted average shares—diluted	6,361	6,368	6,317

(See notes to Consolidated Financial Statements, which are an integral part of these statements.)

EXHIBIT 5.4

PFIZER INC. AND SUBSIDIARY COMPANIES CONTINUED

Consolidated Statement of Income

	December 31	
	2001	**2000**
	(in millions, except per share data)	
ASSETS		
Current assets		
Cash and cash equivalents	$ 1,036	$ 1,099
Short-term investments	7,579	5,764
Accounts receivable, less allowance for doubtful accounts: 2001, $145; 2000, $151	5,337	5,489
Short-term loans	269	140
Inventories		
Finished goods	1,185	1,195
Work in process	1,095	1,074
Raw materials and supplies	461	433
Total inventories	2,741	2,702
Prepaid expenses and taxes	1,488	1,993
Total current assets	18,450	17,187
Long-term loans and investments	5,729	2,529
Property, plant and equipment, less accumulated depreciation	10,415	9,425
Goodwill, less accumulated amortization: 2001, $358; 2000, $300	1,722	1,791
Other assets, deferred taxes, and deferred charges	2,837	2,578
Total assets	$ 39,153	$ 33,510
LIABILITIES AND SHAREHOLDERS EQUITY		
Current liabilities		
Short-term borrowings, including current portion of long-term debt	$ 6,265	$ 4,289

EXHIBIT 5.4

Pfizer Inc. and Subsidiary Companies continued

	December 31	
	2001	**2000**
	(in millions, except per share data)	
Accounts payable	1,579	1,719
Dividends payable	819	696
Income taxes payable	806	850
Accrued compensation and related items	1,083	982
Other current liabilities	3,088	3,445
Total current liabilities	13,640	11,981
Long-term debt	2,609	1,123
Postretirement benefit obligation other than pension plans	587	564
Deferred taxes on income	452	380
Other noncurrent liabilities	3,572	3,386
Total liabilities	20,860	17,434
Shareholders' equity		
Preferred stock, without par value; 12 shares authorized, none issued	—	—
Common stock, $.05 par value; 9,000 shares authorized; issued: 2001 - 6,792; 2000 - 6,749	340	337
Additional paid-in capital	9,300	8,895
Retained earnings	24,430	19,599
Accumulated other comprehensive expense	(1,749)	(1,515)
Employee benefit trusts	(2,650)	(3,382)
Treasury stock, shares at cost: 2001 - 515; 2000 - 435	(11,378)	(7,858)
Total shareholders equity	18,293	16,076
Total liabilities and shareholders equity	$ 39,153	$ 33,510

(See notes to Consolidated Financial Statements which are an integral part of these statements.)

EXHIBIT 5.4

PFIZER INC. AND SUBSIDIARY COMPANIES CONTINUED

Consolidated Statement of Cash Flows

	Year ended December 31		
	2001	**2000**	**1999**
			(in millions)
OPERATING ACTIVITIES			
Income from continuing operations	$ 7,752	$ 3,718	$ 4,972
Adjustments to reconcile income from continuing operations to net cash provided by operating activities:			
Depreciation and amortization	1,068	968	905
Gains on sales of equity investments	(17)	(216)	—
Harmonization of accounting methodology	(175)	—	—
Loss on sale of Animal Health feed-additive products	—	85	—
Costs associated with the withdrawal of Rezulin	—	102	—
Trovan inventory write-off	—	—	310
Deferred taxes and other	217	(265)	213
Changes in assets and liabilities, net of effect of businesses divested:			
Accounts receivable	(30)	(498)	(1,274)
Inventories	(102)	(436)	(278)
Prepaid and other assets	132	365	(127)
Accounts payable and accrued liabilities	(201)	807	378
Income taxes payable	298	1,315	144
Other deferred items	349	250	250
Net cash provided by operating activities	9,291	6,195	5,493

EXHIBIT 5.4

PFIZER INC. AND SUBSIDIARY COMPANIES CONTINUED

	Year ended December 31		
	2001	**2000**	**1999**
			(in millions)
INVESTING ACTIVITIES			
Purchases of property, plant and equipment	(2,203)	(2,191)	(2,493)
Proceeds from disposals of property, plant and equipment	68	91	83
Purchases of short-term investments, net of maturities	(14,218)	(7,982)	(9,270)
Proceeds from redemptions of short-term investments	12,808	6,592	7,785
Purchases of long-term investments	(3,713)	(618)	(40)
Proceeds from sales of equity investments	80	346	42
Increases in long-term loans	—	(220)	(41)
Purchases of other assets	(242)	(174)	(253)
Proceeds from sales of other assets	137	184	193
Proceeds from sales of businesses—net	8	193	26
Other investing activities	50	26	62
Net cash used in investing activities	(7,225)	(3,753)	(3,906)
FINANCING ACTIVITIES			
Proceeds from issuances of long-term debt	1,837	18	14,025
Repayments of long-term debt	(151)	(529)	(14,046)
Increase in short-term debt	2,351	1,247	2,134
Decrease in short-term debt	(526)	(2,427)	(14)
Proceeds from common stock issuances	62	59	62
Purchases of common stock	(3,665)	(1,005)	(2,542)
Cash dividends paid	(2,715)	(2,197)	(1,820)

EXHIBIT 5.4

PFIZER INC. AND SUBSIDIARY COMPANIES CONTINUED

	Year ended December 31		
	2001	**2000**	**1999**
			(in millions)
Stock option transactions and other	711	1,129	574
Net cash used in financing activities	(2,096)	(3,705)	(1,627)
Net cash used in discontinued operations	(28)	—	(20)
Effect of exchange-rate changes on cash and cash equivalents	(5)	4	11
Net decrease in cash and cash equivalents	(63)	(1,259)	(49)
Cash and cash equivalents at beginning of year	1,099	2,358	2,407
Cash and cash equivalents at end of year	$ 1,036	$ 1,099	$ 2,358
SUPPLEMENTAL CASH FLOW INFORMATION			
Cash paid during the period for:			
Income taxes	$ 1,006	$ 1,041	$ 1,573
Interest	303	460	379

(See notes to Consolidated Financial Statements, which are an integral part of these statements.)

Source: Pfizer Company 2001 annual report.

Cash Flow Adequacy Ratio

The cash flow adequacy ratio looks at the adequacy of the cash left, after taxes, interest, and capital expenditures, for covering the company's debt.

$$\text{Cash flow adequacy ratio} = \frac{\text{EBITDA} - \text{Taxes paid} - \text{Interest paid} - \text{Capital expenditures}}{\text{Average annual debt maturities scheduled over the next five years}}$$

Once again, Pfizer has improved its position. According to Mills and Yamamura, the cash flow adequacy ratio reflects credit quality. Pfizer can be perceived as having improved its credit quality.

The eight ratios discussed above may not be widely available as industry averages. However, their use could be made very relevant by company results for comparable companies in the same industry or by examining a company's trends over the years, as we did for two years for Pfizer above.

Other Approaches to Cash Flow Analysis

The previous analyses of cash flow ratios focus on one thing at a time. Another approach enables one to see the big picture. Percentage analysis (similar to common-size statements) of a cash flow statement reports the dollar amounts in terms of percentages. This enables one to examine trends and unusual results. The base-year-to-date approach (1999 being the base year) shows the percentage increase from 1999 to 2000 and from 1999 to 2001 for Coca-Cola Company. Drastic changes are highlighted in this type of analysis and point out the types of line items that may be less predictable in the future (and therefore riskier). The year-to-year approach shows how much each year changes from the year right before it. Horizontal analysis compares one year to another, whereas vertical analysis focuses on one particular year and shows every component of a cash flow statement as a percentage of a summary amount. This vertical analysis gives an indication of the magnitude of each line item's contribution to the big picture. For example, in 2001, the cash flow from operations was 51.5 percent of the total cash inflows for the year.

Other Common-Size Statements

A common-size income statement is a very efficient way to take in a lot of information about earnings at once. Everything is expressed as a percentage of sales or operating revenues. So the first line is 100 percent, and everything below is a percentage of that. An analysis like this helps one to focus on what may be unusual for the company so that anything appearing to detract from the quality of the earnings can be further investigated.

The common-size balance sheet is presented to round out the picture. Everything on the balance sheet is also presented as a percentage of the sales for that year.

Using Free Cash Flow to Examine Company Value

Free cash flow may be more predictive of future potential success than is net income, although the conventional wisdom is that historical net income is better for predicting future cash flows. Net income can be manipulated somewhat by delaying the write-off of bad debts, increasing the estimated useful life of assets or reclassifying trading investments as available-for-sale investments, to name just a few examples. Free cash flow is less subject to judgment, and its analysis can be a useful addition to the tools used to analyze the financial picture of a company.

Free cash flow is typically defined as cash flow from operations minus capital expenditures. This result represents the remaining resources that are available for creditors (to pay interest and pay off loans) and owners (to pay dividends). For GE, information from the cash flow statement shows the following:

	2001	2000
Cash from operating activities (in millions)	$32,195	$22,690
Additions to property, plant and equipment	(15,520)	(13,967)
Dispositions of prop., plant and equipment	7,345	6,767
Payments for principal businesses purchased	(12,429)	(2,332)
Free cash flow	$11,591	$13,158

TIPS & TECHNIQUES

One-Step Approach to Price-Per-Share

A one-step approach to the analysis described above would involve the following equation:

$$\frac{\text{(Stock price/share} \times \text{number of shares) + Debt}}{\text{Cash flow}} = \text{An expected multiple}$$

and the following steps:

1. Locate the number of shares in a note about EPS
2. Locate the debt in the balance sheet
3. Locate the cash flow in the cash flow statement
4. Identify a relevant multiple (through Internet resources and/or financial press outlets)

Plug it all in as follows:

$$\frac{\text{(Stock price per share} \times \text{9,932 million) + \$434,984}}{\text{\$26,800}} = \text{35 times}$$

and solve for "stock price per share."

Two items from the "Cash flows—investing activities" section are not included above because they relate to loans with customers and purchases of securities.

The next question one might ask is, "Can the value of the company be justified by the cash flow situation?" Or, "What is the relationship between the cash flows of the company and its market value?" Or, "Is the stock price reasonable?"

To arrive at the company's market value, a traditional method is to add the market capitalization (current stock price × number of shares outstanding) and the debt. For GE, the market capitalization, using the stock price on May 22, 2002, is

$31.62/share × 9,932 million shares outstanding = $314,050 million

TIPS & TECHNIQUES

Analysts do the types of calculations found in analyses of cash flow all the time, and they seem to do it, sometimes, in real time, since websites like Multex.com display updated results of ratio comparisons every day. One of the best shortcuts to company information on the Internet is to obtain the ticker symbol (e.g., in *The Wall Street Journal*) and do a word search on the ticker symbol. If you found results like the following, the stock price might seem to be justified:

	Company	Industry	Sector	S&P 500
Price to sales	1.34	1.16	1.16	1.78
Price to book	3.01	2.71	2.71	2.61
Price to tangible book	7.09	7.42	7.42	4.07
Price to cash flow	7.83	8.40	8.40	10.63
Price to free cash flow	16.63	16.78	16.78	18.88

The total company value is the sum of the market capitalization and the debt.

$314,050 million + $434,984 million = $749,034 million

Relating the value of the company to the free cash flow calculated for 2001 above, we get a multiple of 64.62:

$749,034 million/$11,591 million = 64.62

Such a multiple seems high for the industry and the sector. Notice that the calculation of free cash flow above begins with cash from operating activities, which itself begins with net income. Some would say that

IN THE REAL WORLD

Free Cash Flow

Free cash flow can be defined as cash from operations, minus dividends and capital expenditures. The idea of a cash flow seems straightforward since cash flows are so readily identified and net cash flow is the difference between cash inflows and cash outflows. However, free cash flow excludes certain information, such as acquisitions of certain assets. Anytime a number or piece of information can exclude something, it is subject to manipulation simply by structuring transactions or situations in a way that will enable that information to be "ignored," so to speak. For example, Tyco treated certain purchases of customer contracts as acquisitions, enabling the company to exclude payments for the contracts from its definition of free cash flow. The result seems to be the omission of information that could be important to investors' decisions.

Source: "How Is Tyco Accounting for Its Cash Flow?" *The Wall Street Journal*, March 5, 2002, C1–C2.

net income is more inclusive of things tangential to operations and that earnings before interest and taxes (EBIT) is more focused on operations. So, a revision of free cash flow is:

EBIT	$30,763
+ Depreciation and amortization	7,089
+ Net change in current accounts	12,582
+ Provision for losses on financing receivables	2,481
– All other	(5,511)
	$47,404
Additions to property, plant and equipment	(15,520)
Dispositions of property, plant and equipment	7,345
Payments for businesses	(12,429)
Revised free cash flow	$26,800

The multiple of company value to revised free cash flow decreases, as follows:

$749,034 million/$26,800 million = 27.95

If an investor believed that a multiple of 35 was appropriate, then a total company value of $938,000 million would be expected. Removing the debt of $434,984 million would leave an expected equity value of $503,016 million.

$938,000 million – $434,984 million = $503,016 million

Finally, on a per share basis, the expected market value would be $50.65.

$503,016 million/9,932 million shares = $50.65 per share

The result could be viewed as a stock price that might be perceived to be justified based on the operations of the company. Anything less would possibly signal an undervalued stock.

IN THE REAL WORLD

When Financial Analysis May Signal Fraud or Earnings Manipulation

Messod D. Beneish developed five indexes that could be useful indicators of earnings manipulation. Four of the five are summarized here, along with the averages for nonmanipulators and manipulators (companies that had manipulated their financial statement numbers):

Index	Formula	Nonmanipulator's Average	Manipulator's Average
I. Days' Sales in Receivables Index	$\dfrac{(\text{Accounts receivable}_t / \text{Sales}_t)}{(\text{Accounts receivable}_{t-1} / \text{Sales}_{t-1})}$	1.031	1.465
II. Gross Margin Index	$\dfrac{((\text{Sales}_{t-1} - \text{Cost of Sales}_{t-1}) / \text{Sales}_{t-1})}{((\text{Sales}_t - \text{Cost of Sales}_t) / \text{Sales}_t)}$	1.014	1.193

III. Asset Quality Index	$\frac{(\text{Current assets}_t + \text{Net fixed assets}_t) / \text{Total assets}_t}{(\text{Current assets}_{t-1} + \text{Net fixed assets}_{t-1}) / \text{Total assets}_{t-1}}$	1.039	1.254
IV. Sales Growth Index	$\frac{\text{Sales}_t}{\text{Sales}_{t-1}}$	1.134	1.607

t: The current year.

t – 1: The previous year.

Sources for Asset Quality Index: "The Detection of Earnings Manipulation," *Financial Analysts Journal*, Sept./Oct. 1999; "International Ratios," *Journal of Accountancy*, August 2001, 80–83.

Summary

The quality of earnings and of financial reporting in general has been of interest for quite a while. The Enron disaster, followed by more and more companies being scrutinized for possible instances of similar inadequate reporting, and the sheer number of recent Securities and Exchange Commission (SEC) required restatements of financial statements, have illustrated the need to keep improving the quality. In fact, the American Accounting Association has sponsored a "Quality of Earnings" project encompassing numerous publications and conferences.[3] A lot of time and effort is being put forth on behalf of decision makers who rely on financial reporting.

CHAPTER 6

Earnings Releases and EVA Analysis

After reading this chapter, you will be able to

- Understand how pro forma statements are created
- Know how pro forma statements are used to add useful information
- Realize how pro forma statements are used to deceive investors in earnings press releases
- Understand how some accounting procedures are felt to distort earnings measures
- Modify earnings to remove the distorting effect of dysfunctional accounting methods
- Calculate and use a company's economic value added (EVA)

Published financial statements are prepared using historical costs and generally accepted accounting principles (GAAP) to measure the amounts involved, and can be expected to universally follow the forms and regulations of the Securities and Exchange Commission (SEC). However, accounting methods are believed to be misleading by some. Financial information is modified or customized to present a "better" message than traditional financial statements in several ways. This chapter discusses alternate presentation in pro forma statements and economic value added (EVA).

Pro Forma Financial Statements

Pro forma or "as if" financial statements are not based on historical costs and/or do not adhere to GAAP or the guidelines of the SEC. Pro forma statements may be prepared, for example, using GAAP but with forecasted amounts, rather than historical costs. In some situations, pro forma statements are required by GAAP or the SEC as, for example, following a consolidation joining two or more companies into one. Finally, companies may use pro forma statements to illustrate for investors and analysts what earnings might have been except for nonrecurring, one-time events, such as an expensive corporate restructuring. The SEC has been critical of pro forma earnings estimates released to analysts and investors by companies that ultimately prove misleading or even fraudulent.

Pro Forma Statements In Budgeting

Budgeted pro forma financial statements are frequently the capstone of the master budget and the culmination of the budgeting cycle. The budgeting process usually begins with a sales forecast. From the sales forecast, operating managers can forecast the labor, materials, and other costs that will be required to provide the product both to be sold and to support desired inventory levels. Sales and production activity drives the activity of other departments or functions and enables those managers to plan their activities and the cash flows associated with those activities. Ultimately, all business units will have forecast their activities and cash flows, and the output of all those budgetary efforts will be summarized in pro forma financial statements prepared for the period. The pro forma statements give managers a preview of how published financial statements will appear if actual activities, revenues, and costs are as budgeted.

Because it is extremely unlikely that actual results will match budgeted results, budgeted schedules can be usefully altered to see what pro forma statements alternative conditions produce.

- "What if raw material prices increase by 10 percent?"
- "What if the union succeeds in getting its proposed wage package approved?"
- "What if the economy worsens and sales decline by 10?" "By 15 percent?"

The budget schedules can be changed to reflect each of these possibilities and show its effect on the financial statements.

Pro Forma Income Statement with Sales Decreasing
(000 omitted)

	Budgeted Sales 70,000 Units	Sales Decreased 10% 63,000 Units	Sales Decreased 15% 59,500 Units
Sales	$210,000	$189,000	$178,500
Cost of sales	70,000	63,000	59,500
Gross margin	$140,000	$126,000	$119,000
Operating costs	122,000	118,000	116,000
Operating profit	$ 18,000	$ 8,000	$ 3,000

Pro Forma Statements and the SEC

Just as pro forma statements are useful presentations of budgeted or forward-looking performance, there are situations in which pro forma statements of past results are necessary to give perspective to current operations. Pro forma presentations are useful when there is a change in accounting that makes comparing current year performance measured using a revised accounting method with historical results measured using the old method. In such cases, pro forma amounts are calculated assuming retroactive application of the new accounting method, and key figures for prior years are shown as they would have been had the newly adopted principle been in effect.

For example, Sony Corporation changed its method of accounting for stock-based compensation in its 2001 annual report. Because of the change, earnings and earnings per share (EPS) published in 2001 are not comparable with prior years. Using these two amounts prepared by different methods to analyze the trend of earnings and EPS might give rise to misleading results. Exhibit 6.1 contains an excerpt from the notes to Sony's 2001 financial statements showing "as reported" and "pro forma" amounts for three years to enable financial statement readers to understand the effect of the change on operation results.

The SEC Regulation S-X lists a number of situations in which a company is required to include pro forma information in its published annual and quarterly reports and its Form 10K and 10Q. These situations, excerpted from Regulation S-X are shown in Tips & Techniques, "Excerpt from SEC Regulation S-X".

IN THE REAL WORLD

The SEC describes the objective of pro forma statements or amounts in its regulation S-X as follows:

> Pro forma financial information should provide investors with information about the continuing impact of a particular transaction by showing how it might have affected historical financial statements if the transaction had been consummated at an earlier time. Such statements should assist investors in analyzing the future prospects of the registrant because they illustrate the possible scope of the change in the registrant's historical financial position and results of operations caused by the transaction.

EXHIBIT 6.1

Sony Corporation Notes Presenting Pro Forma Results For A Change In Stock-Based Compensation

In accordance with FAS No. 123 "Accounting for Stock-Based Compensation", Sony has elected to account for stock-based compensation under the provisions of APB No. 25 for both the warrant and convertible bond plans. Had compensation for Sony's warrant and convertible bond plans been recognized based on the fair value on the grant date under the methodology prescribed by FAS No. 123, Sony's net income and net income per share for the years ended March 31, 1999, 2000 and 2001 would have been impacted as shown in the following table:

	Year ended March 31			
	1999	2000	2001	2001
	Yen in millions			Dollars in millions
Income before cumulative effect of accounting changes:				
As reported	¥179,004	¥121,835	¥121,227	$970
Pro forma	178,505	121,191	118,524	948
Net income				
As reported	¥179,004	¥121,835	¥16,754	$134
Pro forma	178,505	121,191	14,051	112
	Yen in millions			Dollars in millions
Income before cumulative effect of accounting changes:				
—Basic EPS:				
As reported	¥218.43	¥144.58	¥132.64	$1.06
Pro forma	217.82	143.82	129.69	1.04
—Diluted EPS:				
As reported	195.51	131.70	124.36	0.99
Pro forma	194.97	131.02	121.64	0.97
Net income				
—Basic EPS:				
As reported	¥218.43	¥144.58	¥18.33	$0.15
Pro forma	217.82	143.82	15.37	0.12
—Diluted EPS:				
As reported	195.51	131.70	19.28	0.15
Pro forma	194.97	131.02	16.56	0.13

Source: Sony 2001 annual report, p 122.

TIPS & TECHNIQUES

Excerpt from SEC Regulation S-X

Situations in which a Company Is Required to Publish Pro Forma Information

Article 11-Pro Forma Financial Information

Presentation Requirements

Reg. § 210.11-01.

(a) Pro forma financial information shall be furnished when any of the following conditions exists:

(1) Following the fiscal year or subsequent interim period for which a balance sheet is required for a significant business combination.

(2) Securities being registered by the registrant are to be offered to the security holders of a significant business to be acquired or when the proceeds from the offered securities will be applied directly or indirectly to the purchase of a specific significant business;

(3) The disposition of a significant portion of a business has occurred or is probable and is not fully reflected in the financial statements of the registrant included in the filing;

(4) The company has acquired real estate operations or properties, which in the aggregate are significant.

(5) Pro forma financial information required in connection with a roll-up transaction.

(6) The company previously was a part of another entity and such presentation is necessary to reflect operations and financial position of the company as an autonomous entity; or

(7) Consummation of other events or transactions has occurred or is probable for which disclosure of pro forma financial information would be material to investors.

(b) Omitted.

(c) The pro forma effects of a business combination need not be presented pursuant to this section if separate financial statements of the acquired business are not included in the filing.

Financial statements contain important financial information that is often not apparent from news releases, because some companies put out press releases that use pro forma financial information that is not prepared in accordance with GAAP. GAAP is followed in preparing financial statements to be filed with the SEC. Some pro forma financial information is prepared using methods and principles that are not GAAP and are not acceptable to the SEC.

Preparing and releasing to the press (or otherwise distributing) pro forma statements or amounts not in conformity with GAAP is not illegal or even improper and may help focus investors' attention on critical portions the company's operation. Exhibit 6.2 shows pro forma amounts developed by Curtiss-Wright Corporation and contained in the notes to its 2000 annual report. Curtiss-Wright recalculates key amounts pertaining to several one-time, unusual events. Curtiss-Wright explains the pro forma amounts to financial statement readers and describes the pro forma earnings as "normalized." Financial statement readers who try to estimate the trend in Curtiss-Wright's performance will find the normalized, pro forma earnings more useful than the reported earnings that reflect the impact of the unusual events.

Pro Forma Information in Press Releases

Pro forma amounts or statements in company press releases can be misleading and are sometimes intended to deceive. The SEC has prepared several releases urging investors to be skeptical of pro forma amounts or statements, particularly when the pro forma amounts are not clearly reconciled to the audited annual report published by the company. This is true for pro forma earnings released to the press separate from the company's published financial statements. Investors should read and understand a company's financial results. Investors can access the SEC Web site and download a company's annual report filed on its Form 10K and its

EXHIBIT 6.2

Pro Forma Earnings in Curtiss-Wright Financial Statement Notes

Results of Operations

Curtiss-Wright Corporation posted consolidated net sales of $329.6 million and net earnings of $41.1 million, or $4.03 per diluted share, for the year ended December 31, 2000. Sales for the current year increased 12% over 1999 sales of $293.3 million, and 32% over 1998 sales of $249.4 million. Net earnings for 2000 improved 5% over prior year net earnings of $39.0 million, or $3.82 per diluted share and 41% over net earnings of 1998, which totaled $29.1 million, or $2.82 per diluted share. Net earnings for all three years include several nonrecurring items, which impact a year-to-year comparison. The following table depicts the Corporation's "normalized" results, which should present a clearer picture of its after-tax performance.

Normalized Net Earnings

	2000	**1999**	**1998**
	(in thousands, except for share data)		
Net earnings	$41,074	$39,045	$29,053
Environmental insurance settlements, net	(1,894)	(7,354)	(1,754)
Postretirement benefits and postemployment costs, net	(1,336)	—	—
Facility consolidation costs	50	2,351	518
Gain on sale of nonoperating property	(894)	—	—
Recapitalization costs	910	—	—
Normalized net earnings	$37,910	$34,042	$27,817
Normalized net earnings per diluted share	$ 3.72	$ 3.33	$ 2.70

Source: Curtiss-Wright 2000 annual report, p. 20.

quarterly report filed on its 10Q. The SEC Web site is *www.sec.gov* and its database of corporate filings is at *www.sec.gov/edgar.shtml*.

The SEC advises that investors ask the following questions when they consider relying on pro forma statements or amounts:

- *What is the company assuming?* Pro forma financial results can be misleading, particularly if they change a loss to a profit or hide a significant fact. For example, they may assume that a proposed transaction that benefits the company has actually occurred. Alternatively, they may fail to account for costs or charges. Be sure to look behind the numbers and find out what assumptions the numbers are based on.[1]
- *What is the company not saying?* Be particularly wary when you see pro forma financial results that address only one component of a company's financial results—for example, earnings before interest, taxes, depreciation, and amortization (EBITDA). These kinds of statements can be misleading unless the company clearly describes what transactions are omitted and how the numbers might compare to other periods.
- *How do the pro forma results compare with GAAP-based financials?* Because pro forma information comes from selective editing of financial information compiled in accordance with GAAP, pro

IN THE REAL WORLD

Intentionally Deceptive?

In October of 2001, Enron issued an earnings press release that described $1.1 billion of expenses and losses as "nonrecurring charges" so the amounts would not be subtracted in calculating operating earnings and thus issue a pro forma earnings that supported the price of its stock. Enron, when examined by Anderson using its fraud analysis techniques, was identified as "red alert: a heightened risk of financial fraud."

forma financial results can raise a serious risk of misleading investors—even if they do not change a loss to a profit. Look for a clear, comprehensible explanation of how pro forma results differ from financial statements prepared under GAAP rules, and make sure you understand any differences before investing based on pro forma results.

- *Are you reading pro forma results or a summary of GAAP-based financials?* Remember that there is a big difference between pro forma financial information and a summary of a financial statement that has been prepared in accordance with GAAP. When financial statements have been prepared in compliance with regular accounting rules, a summary of that information can be quite useful, giving you the overall picture of a company's financial position without the mass of details contained in the full financial statements. It is always best, however, to compare any summary financial presentation you read with the full GAAP-based financial statements.

Misleading Pro Forma Earnings Enforcement Action

In 2002, the SEC brought its first pro forma earnings case against Trump Hotels and Casino Resorts, Inc., for misleading statements in its 1999 third-quarter earnings release. Trump issued a press release that cited net income and EPS that differed from net income and EPS determined using GAAP. The SEC said that the Trump case "illustrates how pro forma numbers can be used deceptively and the mischief that they can cause,"[2] and that its chief financial officer (CFO) had violated the antifraud regulations of the Securities and Exchange Act by "knowingly or recklessly issuing a materially misleading press release."

The problem resulted when Trump, first, noted that its figures excluded the one-time charge, which implies that there are no other one-time items included in the figures, and then—without comment—including an unusual, one-time gain. As a result, Trump released pro forma earnings that were primarily the result of a one-time, unusual gain instead of from operations, as was implied. Although Trump did not use the term *pro forma,* the figures were pro forma in that the one-time gain was excluded.

The press release stated that Trump's net income and EPS included in the release excluded a $84.4 million one-time charge. The press release did not inform readers that earnings did include an undisclosed one-time gain of $17.2 million. All revenue (including the gain) was on a single line, further giving the impression that the revenue was all from operations. Further, Trump's chief executive officer (CEO) was quoted in the press release as stating that Trump's improved results (from the previous year) came from improvements in operations.

The total effect of unusual items included in Trump's 1999 third-quarter earnings was

One-time gain (included in income)	$17,200,000
One-time loss (excluded from income)	$84,400,000
Total effect of unusual events	($67,200,000)

Exhibit 6.3 contains the earnings statement published in Trump's third-quarter 1999 Form 10Q filed with the SEC. The published financial statements comply with GAAP and the SEC. Consequently, Trump shows a loss of $67,470,000 for the third quarter of 1999. After removing the one-time charge (and its tax savings), but including the one-time gain, Trump released earnings of approximately $14 million—a nice improvement over the $5,312,000 earned in the third quarter of 1998.

Exhibit 6.4 contains excerpts from Trumps Form 10Q documenting the one-time, unusual items in Management's Discussion and Analysis of Financial Condition and Results of Operations, and the notes to the financial statements.

If the impact of both unusual items had been excluded from Trump's pro forma statements, there would have been a decline in revenues and net income. Trump's earnings would not have met analyst's expectations and the price of its stock would have been adversely affected. As it was,

EXHIBIT 6.3

Trump Hotels & Casino Resorts, Inc.

Condensed Consolidated Statements of Operations from Trump's 1999 10Q (unaudited)

	Three Months Ended September 30,		Nine Months Ended September 30,	
	1998	1999	1998	1999
			(dollars in thousands)	
REVENUE:				
Gaming	$ 364,172	$ 350,308	$ 971,945	$ 972,529
Rooms	26,841	28,569	70,930	72,262
Food and Beverage	40,927	40,429	110,443	109,523
Other	13,132	30,902	33,556	51,442
Gross Revenues	445,072	450,208	1,186,874	1,205,756
Less—Promotional allowances	47,685	47,136	128,578	125,522
Net Revenues	397,387	403,072	1,058,296	1,080,234
COSTS AND EXPENSES:				
Gaming	220,846	210,945	607,901	598,238
Rooms	8,470	8,930	23,739	26,177
Food and Beverage	13,989	14,901	38,199	40,175
General and Administrative	70,536	70,213	200,548	209,212
Depreciation and Amortization	21,058	21,041	62,657	63,367
Trump World's Fair Closing Costs	–	128,375	–	128,375
	34,899	454,405	933,044	1,065,544
Income (loss) from operations	62,488	(51,333)	125,252	14,690

EXHIBIT 6.3

TRUMP HOTELS & CASINO RESORTS, INC. CONTINUED

	Three Months Ended September 30,		Nine Months Ended September 30,	
	1998	**1999**	**1998**	**1999**
NONOPERATING INCOME AND (EXPENSES):				
Interest income	2,019	1,833	7,166	5,143
Interest expense	(55,390)	(55,876)	(166,679)	(166,781)
Other nonoperating expense	—	(259)	(286)	(1,719)
	(53,371)	(54,302)	(159,799)	(163,357)
Income (Loss) before equity in loss of Buffington Harbor, LLC, minority interest, and cumulative effect of change in accounting principle	9,117	(105,635)	(34,547)	(148,667)
Equity in loss of Buffington Harbor	(742)	(734)	(2,225)	(2,246)
Income (Loss) before minority interest and cumulative effect of change in accounting principle	8,375	(106,369)	(36,772)	(150,913)
Minority Interest	(3,063)	38,899	13,434	55,189
Income (Loss) before cumulative effect of change in accounting principle	5,312	(67,470)	(23,338)	(95,724)
Cumulative effect of change in accounting principle ($5,620), net of minority interest ($2,055)	—	—	—	(3,565)
NET INCOME (LOSS)	$ 5,312	$ (67,470)	$ (23,338)	$ (99,289)

EXHIBIT 6.4

Trump One-Time Items as Explained in Its 10Q

Management's Discussion and Analysis of Financial Condition and Results of Operations

On September 15, 1999, an agreement was reached between Taj Associates, All Star and Planet Hollywood International, Inc., to terminate the All Star Café Lease effective September 24, 1999. Upon termination of the All Star Cafe Lease, all improvements, alterations and All Star's personal property with the exception of Specialty Trade Fixtures became the property of Taj Associates. Specialty Trade Fixtures, which included signs, emblems, logos, memorabilia and other material with logos of the Official All Star Cafe presently displayed at the premises, could be continued to be used by Taj Associates for a period of up to 120 days without charge. Taj Associates recorded the estimated fair market value of these assets in other revenue based on an independent appraisal in the amount of $17,200,000.

Form 10Q Financial Statement
Note (7) Trump World's Fair Closing

On October 4, 1999, THCR closed Trump World's Fair. The estimated cost of closing Trump World's Fair is $128,375,000 which includes $97,682,000 for the writedown of the assets and $30,693,000 of costs incurred and to be incurred in connection with the closing and demolition of the building.

Trump's stock rose 7.8 percent in response to the press release. Three days later, an analyst's report and a newspaper article informed investors of the one-time gain, and Trump's stock fell 6.0 percent.

Pro Forma Forecasts Following Regulation S-X

It is useful to note that the SEC allows companies to publish forecasted pro forma financial statements or amounts under certain limited conditions following specific rules contained in regulation S-X.

The EVA Approach to Measuring "Real" Earnings

Some investors and analysts argue that GAAP/SEC-compliant earnings are intended for use primarily by creditors, and, because of this, the accounting principle of conservatism leads accountants to paint the most pessimistic picture of the company's earnings and financial position. To some extent, this position is difficult to criticize.

Assets shown at historical cost are often ridiculously undervalued. A parcel of land purchased in downtown Cleveland in 1902 is shown on today's balance sheet at its $500 1902 purchase price, despite the indisputable truth that the parcel is worth millions today. In financial statements the cost of advertising and new product research are treated as immediate expenses, despite the agreement of everyone involved that these costs benefit the company in the future—which is the working definition of an asset.

Financial statements produced under provisions of GAAP and the SEC report profits intended to tell creditors the amount of earnings and assets available to pay debts under the most pessimistic interpretations. The earnings amounts tell creditors how well protected they are if the company becomes unable to pay its debts. They do not provide investors an impartial assessment of how well the company performed.

There are several approaches to modifying reported net income to make it more meaningful. EVA is a well-known and widely used

IN THE REAL WORLD

Excerpt from SEC Regulation S-X

Situations in which a Company May Publish Pro Forma Forecasts

Article 11-Pro Forma Financial Information

Presentation of Financial Forecast

Reg. § 210.11-03.

(a) A financial forecast may be filed in lieu of the pro forma condensed statements of income.

(1) The financial forecast shall cover a period of at least 12 months from the latest of (i) the most recent balance sheet included in the filing or (ii) the consummation date or estimated consummation date of the transaction.

(2) The forecasted statement of income shall be presented in the same degree of detail as the pro forma condensed statement of income required.

(3) Assumptions particularly relevant to the transaction and effects thereof should be clearly set forth.

(4) Historical condensed financial information of the registrant and the business acquired or to be acquired, if any, shall be presented for at least a recent 12-month period in parallel columns with the financial forecast.

(b) Such financial forecast shall be presented in accordance with the guidelines established by the American Institute of Certified Public Accountants.

(c) Forecasted earnings per share data shall be substituted for pro forma per share data.

(d) This rule does not permit the filing of a financial forecast in lieu of pro forma information required by generally accepted accounting principles.

approach. EVA is a proprietary measure developed by Joel M. Stern and G. Bennett Stewart III, and marketed through Stern Stewart & Company.

Since Stern Stewart first introduced EVA, over 300 companies have used it, including Coca-Cola, Quaker Oats, Boise Cascade, Briggs and

IN THE REAL WORLD

Business Value Added

Management at Brown-Forman Corporation, distillers of Southern Comfort and other spirits, uses an EVA-type measure called Business Value Added (BVA). BVA is geared to increasing stockholders' wealth. The following is taken from Management's Discussion and Analysis in the company's 2001 annual report.

> Brown-Forman's foremost goal is to increase the value of our shareholders' investment. To assist us in achieving this objective, we evaluate performance and compensate our management based on a measure we call Business Value Added (BVA). We define BVA as the company's after-tax operating income less a capital charge for net operating assets employed, recognizing not only the profits generated by the company but also the investment required to produce those profits.
>
> BVA, as defined, grew 9% in fiscal 1999 and 4% in fiscal 2000, and declined 2% in fiscal 2001. These results were affected by a change in U.S. tax regulations, requiring us to repay a $200 million deferred tax liability over a four-year period ending in fiscal 2003. Further, although we expect recent investments in Sonoma-Cutrer and Finlandia will enhance BVA over the long term, these investments have also diluted BVA growth rates. Adjusted for these items, BVA increased 10% in fiscal 1999, 14% in fiscal 2000, and 8% in fiscal 2001.

Source: Brown-Forman Corporation, Annual Report 2001, 19, 20.

Stratton, Lafarge, Siemans, Tate and Lyle, Telstra, Monsanto, JCPenney, and the U.S. Postal Service.[3]

Calculating EVA

Proponents of EVA claim it is a better measure of a company's success than is net income. When people look at an annual report, they are interested in knowing if the company will increase stockholders' wealth. They are not interested in paper profits measured using GAAP. That is why companies issue news releases containing pro forma information. However, even the best pro forma measure of earnings is historical cost based and displays an earnings figure calculated on that basis.

Proponents of EVA argue that investors want to know the company's economic profit—the true amount by which a company is better off. *Equity* is defined as "property rights," of which there are two basic types in accounting: the equity of creditors (liabilities) and the equity of owners (stockholders' equity). EVA is said to measure in real terms the increase in wealth, defined as total equities, including both creditors' equity and stockholders' equity. EVA is the statistic stockholders need. When bonus plans use EVA rather than EPS or return on assets (ROA) to measure the performance of managers, managers pursue activities congruent with the interests of stockholders. Change in EVA is the force that causes change in the market price of a company's stock.

EVA is calculated as:

EVA = NOPAT – (The cost of capital) × (Total debt and owners' equity)

EVA = NOPAT – (WACC) × (L + OE)

Where:

NOPAT = Net operating profit after taxes
WACC = Weighted average cost of capital (as a percentage)
L = Liabilities (the equity of creditors)
OE = Owners' equity

If a company's NOPAT is $5,000 and its total debt and owners' equity are $10,000 with a 10 percent cost of capital, EVA is calculated as

$$EVA = \$5{,}000 - (\$10{,}000 \times 0.10)$$
$$EVA = \$5{,}000 - \$1{,}000$$
$$EVA = \$4{,}000$$

If a company earns only enough to cover its cost of capital, it has earned no profit. Thus, the cost of capital is generally a company's minimum desired rate of return—anything less creates a loss.

To calculate NOPAT, operating profit after tax must be adjusted to correct for accounting distortions caused by GAAP presentation. NOPAT should be called NOPATA—net operating profit after taxes and adjustments. Stern Stewart have identified 120 possible distortions of profit created by accounting procedures, though companies in practice need to correct for only a dozen or so. The accounting treatment of the following items is felt to cause the most egregious distortions of reported profits and its surrogate measures, such as EPS and the price/earnings (P/E) ratio.

- *Historical cost.* Historical cost is a different problem. Assets are shown on the balance sheet at their original purchase cost or at market price, whichever is lower. With even mild inflation, this causes assets to be understated. One of the authors of this book graduated from college in 1963 and started to work at a $6,900 salary. It was a great salary—more than my accounting professor earned at that time. Dollars from the past cannot be mingled with current dollars in calculations. It is like mingling measurements in yards and meters: the results are of only marginal use.
- *Deferred taxes.* Because tax accounting and GAAP accounting have different goals and thus different rules, events (earning revenue, incurring expenses) are often recorded in tax and accounting in different years. Accounting procedures often include as expenses amounts of deferred taxes not currently paid by a company. Deducting deferred, unpaid taxes from income increases expenses and depresses profit and owners' equity. EVA records a tax expense only when it paid.

- *Research and development.* GAAP requires companies to expense the cost of research and development each year, as though the expenditure provides no benefit in future years. EVA proponents argue that expensing research and development both understates a company's assets because it ignores the investment value of this cost and overstates expenses, which drives profits down. From a creditor's point of view (i.e., GAAP) research and development (R&D) is an asset that cannot be turned into cash to pay debts, so why book it? From the investor's point of view, a company's expenditures on R&D are highly correlated with its stock price.
- *Advertising and marketing.* GAAP also requires companies to expense advertising and other selling/marketing costs year by year. No sane businessperson believes that the millions spent on Super Bowl ads have no benefit to the company once the ad has run. Here, too, EVA proponents argue that expensing these costs understates a company's assets, overstates its expenses, and drives profits down.
- *Employee training.* Consultants, professional organizations, and others conduct hundreds of thousands of hours of employee training courses year after year. Many companies have excellent in-house training facilities. It is unrealistic not to recognize that

IN THE REAL WORLD

GE Financial Training

General Electric hires many accounting and finance college graduates for its financial management training tract that consists of several years of combined classroom and on-the-job training. Students compete intensely for these positions, and competitors often pay handsomely to entice these people to leave GE.

training employees benefits the future. As a result, assets and expenses are overstated and profit is understated.

- *Allowances and reserves.* In trying to correctly value assets, liabilities, and owners' equity, accountants create reserves or allowances. When a refrigerator is sold, for instance, the accountant knows the company will eventually spend, say, $75 for warranty costs. Some will have expensive warranty repairs; others will have few, if any, warranty costs. To account for this, and to let investors know the company has incurred this liability, the accountant will expense $75 and establish an allowance for warranty obligations that will be paid in the future. The EVA school of thought says the warranties are not business expenses until the refrigerator is actually repaired under the warranty.

  Often reserves are too large and unnecessarily obscure profits, says former SEC Chairman Arthur Levitt, Jr.[4] He has referred to allowances for warranties, bad debts, discounts taken, and so forth as "cookie jar" reserves. EVA records their expenses only when they are paid.

- *Multiple GAAP accounting methods.* Frequently, there are several methods of accounting for an event and companies must choose among them. Some methods affect taxable income, some do not. More than one method of accounting is available for each of the following very ordinary business activities. The choice made for each affects the amount of earnings and assets a company includes in its financial statements: purchases of inventory, sales of inventory, depreciating assets, estimating bad debts, leases, amortizing intangibles, manufacturing a product, drilling for oil, and accounting for a series of "one-time" events, such as corporate restructuring (a supposed one-time cost that some companies incur every year).

There are several methods acceptable for calculating depreciation expense on assets such as plant and equipment: straight line, double-declining balance, sum-of-the-years digits and activity-based, group, and others. All of these methods result in the same total depreciation expense over the life of the asset involved, but the pattern of the expense over the years is different. In addition, regardless of the depreciation method used for financial reporting, a company is free for tax reporting to use the depreciation method that results in the lowest tax liability. Consequently, the choice of depreciation method for reporting earnings does not result in different cash flows, only in different reported earnings.

The choice of inventory method is different, however. The IRS requires a company to use the same inventory counting method for both financial reporting and taxes. The same is true of accounting for leases

TIPS & TECHNIQUES

Building Ships and Dams

When a company's operations involve long-term projects, such as building a ship or a dam that requires a number of years to complete, the company can use one of two vastly different methods to recognize and report revenue and expenses.

One method, called the *completed contract method*, lets the company wait until the contract is completed to report all the revenue and expenses. This gives the odd pattern of loss, loss, loss . . . then, big profit in the completion year. The alternate method is called the percentage completion method and allows the company to estimate its progress on the project and report that percentage of revenues and expenses each year. When the ship is one-half completed, the company reports one half of the revenues, expenses, and profit. This lets investors and creditors monitor the profit earned each year. Nevertheless, of course, there are several different ways to estimate the percentage completed, which can affect profit recognition.

and some other costs. When the same method must be used for both taxes and financial reporting, the choice impacts cash flows as well as reported profits.

Management's Impact on Reported Profit

Reported profits are also distorted at times by management actions. These effects are divided into two basic types of action: (1) using accepted accounting and business practices to manage earnings, and (2) using unaccepted and sometimes fraudulent methods to effect reported profit. Managers are highly motivated to increase stockholder wealth (which is good). The increase is often part of a business game.

Managers can manage profits in many legal, ethical ways. Managers can change the timing of revenue and expense recognition. For example,

IN THE REAL WORLD

The Moving Target

An often played scene in real business: The board tells the CFO: "Increase profits in the south by 8 percent." The CFO tells the chief operating officer (COO): "Increase profits in the south by 10 percent." The COO tells the southern regional manager: "Increase profits by 15 percent." The southern regional manager tells the sales manager: "Increase profits by 20 percent." And so on. . . .

As a goal travels down the pyramid, it is often increased as each level of management seeks to build in a safety cushion. Even worse, someone in power eventually tells the financial press directly or indirectly what profits are expected. Then, the actual increase must be at least as large as stock market analysts announce. Missing analysts' predictions by a penny can cause a company's stock price to fall.

a store can offer liberal credit terms to entice customers to buy in December rather than wait until next year. A company that advertises "No payment or interest until June" may motivate customers to buy a boat for Christmas instead of waiting until spring. Such shifts in sales increase current-year earnings but steal sales from next year. Earnings in one year are increased, while earnings the next year are reduced.

Often, when managers realize that a year will result in large expenses and a loss, they are motivated to move discretionary expenses and unusual charges (such as a corporate restructuring or the sale of an obsolete plant) to take the "hit" in the same year. This is referred to as the "big bath." The logic is that investors will see the year as an expense cleansing and believe the coming year will be better with all the loss activities cleared from the deck.

Alternatively, managers can change earnings in ways that are more questionable. Managers can increase sales by loosening credit standards. This might increase sales, but in the long run result in increased bad debt losses.

Managers can also fudge expenses that are based on estimates, such as obsolete inventories or warranty costs, delaying recognition of the full amount of these costs. Actions such as these are ethically questionable and result (if successful) in earnings increases in one year at the expense of another as the costs must eventually be written off. Profits created by such questionable practices cannot be sustained and do not provide an accompanying increased inflow of cash or other assets.

Market Value Added

Market value added (MVA) is an offshoot of EVA. MVA looks at the market price of the company's stock to measure the company's equity value. The important metric in MVA is the excess in market value of the company's stock and the amounts invested in it over the years.

MVA is calculated as:

MVA = (Market value of common stock
+ Market value of preferred stock
+ Market value of debt)
− Total capital

There are two different theories involved in MVA and EVA. Proponents of EVA will argue that the market price of a company's stock is based on expectations about the company's performance in the future and that EVA best measures this amount. In contrast, MVA is described as "the present value of future expected EVA."[5]

Estimating EVA from an Annual Report Data

Exhibits 6.5 and 6.6 contain the financial statements and a portion of Note 1 from the 2001 annual report of Brown-Forman Corporation.

EXHIBIT 6.5

Brown-Forman Corporation Annual Report

Income Statement, Balance Sheet, and Statement of Cash Flows for the Year 2001

Year Ended April 30,	**1999**	**2000**	**2001**
	(in millions, except per share amounts)		
Net sales	$ 2,009	$ 2,134	$ 2,180
Excise taxes	254	257	256
Cost of sales	736	774	771
Gross profit	1,019	1,103	1,153
Advertising expenses	263	281	295
Selling, general, and administrative expenses	434	474	484
Operating income	322	348	374
Interest income	6	10	8

EXHIBIT 6.5

BROWN-FORMAN CORPORATION CONTINUED

Year Ended April 30,	1999	2000	2001
Interest expense	10	15	16
Income before income taxes	318	343	366
Taxes on income	116	125	133
Net income	$ 202	$ 218	$ 233
Earning per share—Basic and Diluted	$ 2.93	$ 3.18	$ 3.40
Weighted average shares used to calculate earnings per share:			
Basic	68.6	68.5	68.5
Diluted	68.7	68.6	68.6
Assets			
Cash and cash equivalents	$ 171	$ 180	$ 86
Accounts receivable, less allowance for doubtful accounts of $11 in 1999, $12 in 2000, and $12 in 2001	274	294	303
Inventories:			
Barreled whiskey	191	202	219
Finished goods	189	184	216
Work in process	89	80	93
Raw materials and supplies	56	48	49
Total inventories	525	514	577
Other current assets	29	32	28
Total Current Assets	999	1,020	994
Property, plant, and equipment, net	348	376	424
Intangible assets, less accumulated amortization of $135 in 1999, $146 in 2000, and $156 in 2001	264	270	263
Other assets	124	136	258
Total Assets	$ 1,735	$ 1,802	$ 1,939

EXHIBIT 6.5

BROWN-FORMAN CORPORATION CONTINUED

Year Ended April 30,	1999	2000	2001
Liabilities			
Commercial paper	$ 226	$ 220	$ 204
Accounts payable and accrued expenses	235	271	281
Current portion of long-term debt	18	6	—
Accrued taxes on income	—	1	45
Deferred income taxes	31	15	8
Total Current Liabilities	510	513	538
Long-term debt	53	41	40
Deferred income taxes	137	95	62
Accrued postretirement benefits	57	58	59
Other liabilities and deferred income	61	47	53
Total Liabilities	818	754	752
Stockholders' Equity			
Capital Stock:			
Class A common stock, voting, $0.15 par value; authorized shares, 30,000,000; issued shares, 28,988,091	4	4	4
Class B common stock, nonvoting, $0.15 par value; authorized shares, 60,000,000; issued shares, 40,008,147	6	6	6
Retained earnings	945	1,080	1,226
Cumulative translation adjustment	(8)	(12)	(17)
Treasury stock, at cost (490,000, 484,000, and 537,000 Class B common shares in 1999, 2000, and 2001, respectively)	(30)	(30)	(32)
Total Stockholders' Equity	917	1,048	1,187
Total Liabilities and Stockholders' Equity	$1,735	$1,802	$1,939

Source: Brown-Forman Corporation 2001 annual report, pp. 25–28.

EXHIBIT 6.6

Brown-Forman Corporation Annual Report: Excerpts from Notes 1 and 5 for the Year 2001

Note 1: Accounting Policies

Principles of Consolidation

The consolidated financial statements include the accounts of all majority-owned subsidiaries. Investments in affiliates in which the company has the ability to exercise significant influence, but not control, are accounted for by the equity method. All other investments in affiliates are carried at cost. Intercompany transactions are eliminated.

Cash Equivalents

Cash equivalents include demand deposits with banks and all highly liquid investments with original maturities of three months or less.

Inventories

Inventories are stated at the lower of cost or market. Approximately 85% of consolidated inventories are valued using the last-in, first-out (LIFO) method. All remaining inventories are valued using the first-in, first-out and average cost methods.

If the LIFO method had not been used, inventories would have been $110, $110, and $105 higher than reported at April 30, 1999, 2000, and 2001, respectively.

EXHIBIT 6.6

BROWN-FORMAN CORPORATION ANNUAL REPORT: EXCERPTS FROM NOTES 1 AND 5 CONTINUED

Note 5: Debt

The company's long-term debt consisted of the following:

April 30,	1999	2000	2001
6.82% to 7.38% medium-term notes, due 2005	$ 30	$ 30	$ 30
Variable rate industrial revenue bonds, due through 2026	10	10	10
Other	31	7	—
	71	47	40
Less current portion	18	6	—
	$ 53	$ 41	$ 40

No long-term debt payments are required until fiscal 2006. Cash paid for interest was $11 in 1999, $15 in 2000, and $16 in 2001. The weighted average interest rates on commercial paper were 4.9% at April 30, 1999, 6.1% at April 30, 2000, and 4.8% at April 30, 2001. The weighted average interest rates on variable rate industrial revenue bonds were 4.1%, 5.2%. and 4.3% at April 30, 1999, 2000, and 2001, respectively.

Source: Brown-Forman Corporation 2001 annual report, pp. 30, 31

Exhibit 6.7 contains an estimate of Brown-Forman's EVA at the end of 2001. The EVA calculation is made with only the annual report and thus limited information about other factors that can impact EVA. Additionally, we correct NOPAT based only on the amounts for 2001 and do not try to incorporate factors from earlier years or factors not discussed here.

EXHIBIT 6.7

Brown-Forman Corporation: EVA Calculated Based on 2001 Annual Report Information

EVA = NOPAT – [The cost of capital] × [Total debt and owners' equity]

EVA = NOPAT – (WACC) × (L + OE)

Calculating NOPAT:		
Operating income		$374
Less taxes and distortion items:		
Taxes paid—		
Tax expense IS	133	
Less tax deferred CF	(40)	93
Advertising IS		295
Depreciation CF		53
Amortization CF		11
Allowance for doubtful accounts BS		12
LIFO Reserve (to adjust to current value) From Note 1		105
NOPAT =		$943

Calculating WACC:	
Current liabilities	Amount × Rate = Cost of capital
Commercial paper	$204 × .048 = $ 10 (Note 5)
Accounts payable	281
Accrued taxes on income	45
Deferred income taxes	8
Long-term debt	40 × .071 = 3 (Note 5)

EXHIBIT 6.7

BROWN-FORMAN CORPORATION CONTINUED

Deferred income taxes	62	
Accrued postretirement benefits	59	
Other liabilities and deferred income	53	
Stockholders' equity	1,187 × .120 =	142
Total liabilities and equity	$1,939	$155
WACC =	$155/$1,939 =	.08

EVA = $943 – (.08) × ($1,939) = $1,098

Notes:

The following key identifies the source of amounts used to calculate NOPAT.

IS = income statement

BS = balance sheet

CF = statement of cash flows

All the amounts used in the calculation of WACC are in the balance sheet.

Summary

This chapter covered two very different methods of presenting earnings. Pro forma amounts and financial statements are in the news recently because some companies have released deceptive, even fraudulent, pro forma performance measures in frantic attempts to support the price of their stock. EVA is a proprietary measure used successfully by many large companies to analyze their performance. EVA attempts to calculate the increases in total equities (creditor and owner) each year. A number of adjustments must be made to profits to arrive at NOPAT. This amount minus the cost of capital (creditor and owner) is the equity value added each year. EVA results in a useful calculation of profits and keeps managers focused on increases in shareholder wealth. Market value added (MVA) is a companion to EVA that concentrates on the growth of a company's market value, as opposed to the growth of its equity.

CHAPTER 7

E-Business

After reading this chapter, you will be able to

- Understand the use of the discounted cash flow method of valuation
- Understand the use of the guideline company method of valuation
- Understand various types and uses of price multiples
- Compare the traditional discounted cash flow method and the expected cash flow method

The growth of e-business was phenomenal and apparently outpaced people's ability to invent good ways to make good decisions about those types of businesses. A lot of capital poured into e-business with high hopes of success. A lot of that capital disappeared into a black hole. What looked like good business models were not necessarily accompanied by good valuation models with which to decide whether a return on the investment could be expected. As the industry evolves, stakeholders and decision makers are going back to basics and realizing that maybe profit is the main thing.

Many Internet-related businesses are now publicly held. Many are starting up all the time, aiming to grow and then maybe go public. The kind of information available to decision makers differs between publicly held and privately owned e-businesses. The next section examines some methods for assessing values and returns associated with e-business.

Publicly Held E-Business Companies

Investing in a publicly held Internet-related company is like deciding whether to buy stock in any company. Methods demonstrated in other chapters of this book are appropriate. And comparison of the results with industry and sector averages is also necessary. It is important to identify the appropriate industry for the company under scrutiny. Not every Internet-related business is in the same industry. For example, Amazon.com is in the "retail (specialty)" industry, and eBay is in the "business services" industry. They are both in the services sector. Exhibit 7.1 shows return results for the two companies and their respective industries.

Valuation and E-Business

If you are a business owner making an acquisition decision about an e-business, you can request any number of information items that you think are main value determinants. If you are a wealthy investor approached for venture capital, you can ask whatever questions you want to. If you are a major analyst with a major investment banking firm, you can be in on the conference calls and get interesting and pertinent facts. But if you are a regular, everyday investor, you can get publicly available information only, like the financial statements and Securities and Exchange Commission (SEC) filings. The following approaches for valuation of an e-business for purposes of making an investment in the company's stock are based on the idea that a good basic, maybe even just a preliminary, valuation can be based on the information from an annual report.

EXHIBIT 7.1

Ratio Comparison for Amazon.com and eBay

	eBay	Industry (Business Services)	Amazon.com	Industry (Retail)	Sector	S&P 500
ROA	7.11	7.77	–23.61	5.20	4.86	5.58
ROI	8.01	9.00	–45.69	7.11	6.79	9.16
ROE	8.94	14.98	NA	13.97	10.74	16.42

NA: Not available.

Source: Multex.com, May 2002.

Here is an interesting observation from a study of Intel's press release on September 21, 2000, and the subsequent decline in its stock price:

> The most notable shortcoming is that virtually none of the 28 analyst reports on Intel examined for this study contained a DCF [discounted cash flow] valuation analysis. Furthermore, the few reports that did refer to a DCF value did not present enough information to understand the basis for the calculations. What makes this surprising is that virtually every report contained a recommendation regarding potential purchase or sale of the stock. The mystery is how a purchase recommendation could be offered without an explicit comparison between price and estimated value. From a valuation perspective, attractive securities are those whose price is less than the present value of the expected future cash flows discounted at the appropriate risk-adjusted rate.[1]

There are various approaches to valuation. One categorization can be made as follows:[2]

- Income approach
- Market approach
    - Guideline company method
    - Merger and acquisition method
- Cost approach

The income approach is based on a discounted cash flow (DCF) method. It is a feasible approach to use when one can obtain or estimate, for the subject company, cash flows and discount rates. The market approach is feasible when one can obtain information about some peer companies of the subject company. In particular, the guideline company method can be used with information about revenues, earnings before interest, taxes, depreciation, and amortization (EBITDA) and stock prices of the peer companies, and revenues and EBITDA of the subject company. Therefore, the guideline company method is feasible to use when only annual reports and SEC filings are available, and it will be demonstrated later in the chapter.

The merger and acquisition method is based on comparable transactions between the subject company and peer companies. The subject company's equity is valued using similar sales transactions from peer companies; the more similar the transactions, the better the result. Such information is not available to all.

The cost approach (or net asset approach) depends on knowing the fair value of the individual assets and liabilities of the company. This is not readily available to the regular investor. Furthermore, according to Garruto and Loud, the cost approach may be appropriate when the subject company has a "heavy investment in tangible assets or when operating earnings are insignificant relative to the value of the underlying assets."[3]

Based on the preceding discussion, we will limit our examples of valuation in the above framework to the income approach and the guideline company method of the market approach.

The Discounted Cash Flow Method (Income Approach)

Previous chapters have examined a number of different cash flow streams that could be used in ratio and other kinds of analyses. Such information would be available for publicly traded e-business entities and would in fact be a straightforward performance measure or value indicator for a business that may not yet be making a profit. So a DCF model would provide a relevant perspective on the value of an e-business.

A DCF analysis requires estimates of future performance and/or value (say, cash flows and residual value). It also requires a discount rate, derived by formal model or based on judgment.

The following example is based on a real-life e-business company, which shall remain nameless in order to avoid any appearance of giving advice. Our purpose is merely to demonstrate a method. The DCF method requires certain assumptions, such as projected cash flows, discount rate, and long-term growth rate. Projections here are based on a five-year growth rate included in a research report for this company on the Internet. The discount rate used here is 20 percent to approximate the return an investor might expect from a company in a high-risk industry. The long-term growth rate used is 15 percent because it is the approximate growth rate for the fifth-year projection [($114,488 – $99,885) ÷ $99,885)]. Based on the actual free cash flow at December 31, 2001, and a five-year increase of about 176 percent (given as an estimate in a research report), divided evenly over the five-year period, the projected free cash flows are as shown in Exhibit 7.2.

EXHIBIT 7.2

Discounted Cash Flow Method

Free cash flow	Balance at 12-31-01	Projections of free cash flows at: 12-31-02	12-31-03	12-31-04	12-31-05	12-31-06
	$41,481	$56,082	$70,683	$85,284	$99,885	$114,488

Assumptions: Discount rate = 20%
Long-term growth rate = 15% (the approximate growth in the 5th year)

Residual value (using Gordon Growth Model*)

$$= \frac{\text{Terminal year cash flow} \times (1 + \text{Growth rate})}{\text{Discount rate} - \text{Growth rate}}$$

$$= \frac{\$114,488 \times (1 + .15)}{(.20 - .15)}$$

= $2,633,224

Enterprise value = Present value of residual:

$2,633,224 (.4019) = $1,058,293

+ Present value of cash flows:

$114,488 (.4019)	=	$ 46,013
$ 99,885 (.4823)	=	$ 48,175
$ 85,284 (.5787)	=	$ 49,354
$ 70,683 (.6944)	=	$ 49,082
$ 56,082 (.8333)	=	$ 46,733
Enterprise Value	=	$1,297,650

Equity value = Total value – debt
= $1,297,650 – $124,696 = $1,172,954

Market value per share = $1,172,954/134,486 shares = $8.72/share

Compared to actual stock price = $27.89/share

*See Loren Garruto and Oliver Loud, "Taking the Temperature of Health Care Valuations," *Journal of Accountancy* October 2001, 79–93, for additional discussion of the methods.

The value of the entity is assumed to be the present value of the cash flows plus the present value of the residual, discounted at the desired rate of return. In the example, the value of the entity is calculated to be $1,297,650, but this includes debt of $124,696. So the value of the company's equity is $1,297,650 – $124,696 = $1,172,954. For 134,486 shares, this is an estimated $8.72 per share value for the equity. However, with a current stock price of $27.89 per share, the investor would need to decide whether he or she viewed the stock as overpriced.

Guideline Company Method (Market Approach)

The guideline company method compares the company that needs to be valued with similar companies that are publicly traded. It uses the stock price to determine the total market value of the equity of each guideline company. Then the market value of equity as a percentage of revenues and/or another measure of performance, like EBITDA, is used to estimate a market value for the company being evaluated. Exhibit 7.3 shows the process for six fictitious guideline companies and a subject company. The last two columns, market capitalization to revenues and to EBITDA, are pricing multiples. Once a median pricing multiple is determined for each category (0.325 and 9.45 in our example), this median can be adjusted depending on circumstances. If, for example, the subject company is smaller or less profitable, the multiple may be adjusted downward. Exhibit 7.3 shows different possible pricing multiples and the resulting possible values for the subject company. These values represent the estimate of total company value, so subtract the capital debt (that was included to get market capitalization) and divide the remaining equity value of the subject company by the number of shares outstanding. There, one has an estimate of a reasonable stock price.

EXHIBIT 7.3

Guideline Companies Method

	Revenues*	EBITDA*	EBITDA margin[a]	Market capital to revenues[b]	Market capital to EBITDA[c]
Beachjunk.com	$18,000	$810	.045	0.35	7.8
ClothesandStuff.com	12,000	300	.025	0.25	10.0
Dreammachines.com	14,400	360	.025	0.30	12.0
Desserts.com	30,000	1,050	.035	0.35	10.0
Kit.com	9,000	315	.035	0.20	5.7
Gardens.com	24,000	1,080	.045	0.40	8.0
Median	$16,200		.035	0.325	9.45
Subject company	$4,050	$122	.030		

* In thousands

[a] EBITDA margin = EBITDA/Revenues

[b]Market capital to revenues = $\frac{\text{Stock price} \times \text{\# Shares of stock} + \text{Total capital debt}}{\text{Revenues}}$

[c]Market capital to EBITDA = $\frac{\text{Market capital to revenues}}{\text{EBITDA margin}}$

Possible Values for Subject Company: Selected Multiple Adjustment Factor

Subject company	Pricing multiples =	100% 0.325	100% 9.45	90% .293	90% 8.51	80% 0.260	80% 7.56	70% 0.228	70% 6.62
Revenues =	$4,050	$1,316		$1,187		$1,053		$923	
EBITDA =	$ 122		$1,153		$1,038		$922		$808

If, in our example, we use 80 percent of the price multiple (since the subject company is smaller and less profitable than the median) and average the two results, we get

$$\frac{\$1{,}053{,}000 + \$922{,}000}{2} = \$988{,}000$$

If the value of the capital debt is \$125,000 and there are 75,000 shares outstanding, a reasonable share price is \$11.51.

$$\frac{\$988{,}000 - \$125{,}000}{75{,}000 \text{ shares}} = \$11.51/\text{share}$$

The guideline company method relies on basic price multiples. Multiples based on revenues and EBITDA are especially appropriate for Internet-related companies that may not be profitable yet. The next section summarizes a number of price multiples that may be useful.

The Use of Price Multiples

The value of a company as a whole, or of the stock price of the company, can be estimated or measured in many complicated ways. But the following group of valuation methods uses accounting information usually available to the average investor. So these valuation methods, referred to as price multiples, can be a useful way not only to value companies but also to compare companies and to examine how companies' situations change from one year to the next. Those price multiples are:

$$\text{Price/earnings (P/E) multiples} = \frac{\text{Stock price per share}}{\text{Earnings per share}}$$

$$\text{Price-to-book multiples} = \frac{\text{Stock price per share}}{\text{Book value of equity per share}}$$

$$\text{OR} \quad \text{P/E ratio} \times \text{Earnings-to-equity}$$

$$\text{Price-to-sales multiples} = \frac{\text{Stock price per share}}{\text{Sales revenue per share}}$$

$$\text{OR} \quad \text{P/E ratio} \times \text{Earnings-to-sales}$$

$$\text{Price-to-cash flow multiples} = \frac{\text{Stock price per share}}{\text{Operating cash flow per share}}$$

$$\text{OR} \quad \text{P/E ratio} \times \text{Earnings-to-cash flow}$$

Price/Earnings Ratio. As discussed in Chapter 2, the P/E ratio can be used to assess whether a company is over- or undervalued by the market. Another typical use of the P/E ratio is to assess what the market expects of the company's earnings in the future. A high P/E ratio based on historical data may indicate that the market expects the company to grow in the future. If the P/E ratio is calculated using forecasted EPS and that EPS is lower than the current EPS, then the P/E ratio, based on the lower forecasted EPS (i.e., a lower denominator), will be higher than the current P/E ratio. That higher P/E ratio will then indicate that the market expects a decline in earnings.

To use the P/E ratio to estimate the equity value of a subject Internet company, one would obtain the P/E ratio of one or more comparable companies and multiply the P/E ratio(s) by the earnings of the subject company. The result is an estimate of the subject company's equity value. Any of the other price multiples could be used in a similar way.

$$\text{P/E ratio} = \frac{\text{Stock price per share}}{\text{Earnings per share}}$$

Price-to-Book Ratio. If the market is expecting a substantial growth in the book value of a company, then the price-to-book ratio will be relatively high. A high ratio may also reflect an expectation of high return on equity (ROE) to come. The price-to-book ratio is obviously a comparison of stock price per share and book value per share. However, once the P/E ratio is obtained, the price-to-book ratio is easily calculated as follows:

$$\begin{aligned}\text{Price-to-book ratio} &= \frac{\text{Stock price per share}}{\text{Book value per share}}\\ &= \text{P/E ratio} \times \text{Earnings-to-equity}\\ &= \frac{\text{Stock price per share}}{\text{Earnings per share}} \times \frac{\text{Net income}}{\text{Stockholders' equity}}\end{aligned}$$

Price-to-Sales Ratio. A relatively high price-to-sales ratio could indicate that the market expects a favorable trend in profit margins, or that it has high expectations of the company's profit margins. Again, this ratio can be calculated with a shortcut, derived as follows:

$$\begin{aligned}\text{Price-to-Sales Ratio} &= \frac{\text{Stock price per share}}{\text{Sales revenue per share}} \\ &= \text{P/E ratio} \times \text{Earnings-to-sales} \\ &= \frac{\text{Stock price per share}}{\text{Earnings per share}} \times \frac{\text{Net income}}{\text{Sales revenue}}\end{aligned}$$

Notice that the fraction on the right, above, is basically the profit margin.

Price-to-Cash Flow Ratio. According to Krishna Palepu, Victor L. Bernard, and Paul M. Healy, although the price-to-cash flow ratio would appear to use the information about cash flow from operations, it is better to use EBITDA as a proxy for cash flow from operations. Since cash flow from operations (as reported in the cash flow statement) can be affected by fluctuations in working capital accounts (like accounts receivable, inventory, accounts payable, etc.), that cash flow information might be "a noisy indicator of value as it stands alone."[4] So, one could take the ratio:

$$\begin{aligned}\text{Price-to-cash flow ratio} &= \frac{\text{Stock price per share}}{\text{Operating cash flow per share}} \\ &= \text{P/E ratio} \times \frac{\text{Net income}}{\text{Cash flow from operations}}\end{aligned}$$

and convert it to the following:

$$\text{Price-to-EBITDA} = \text{P/E ratio} \times \frac{\text{Net income}}{\text{EBITDA}}$$

Unlevered Ratios. However, there is one more consideration to make. Ideally, a ratio should contain a numerator that is consistent with the denominator. In the preceding ratio, EBITDA is based on information before the servicing of debt. Therefore, the numerator should also reflect information prior to servicing of debt. So, the price-to-EBITDA ratio should include debt, as follows:

$$\text{Unlevered price-to-EBITDA} = \frac{\text{Market value of equity + Debt}}{\text{EBITDA}}$$

Because the price-to-sales ratio also includes a denominator that is prior to servicing of debt, that ratio can be converted, as follows:

$$\text{Unlevered price-to-sales} = \frac{\text{Market value of equity + Debt}}{\text{Sales}}$$

Exhibit 7.4 shows a summary of the price multiples for Amazon.com and eBay in May 2002 in order to compare them to the sector and Standard & Poor's 500.

Entrepreneurial or Start-up E-Businesses

If an e-business is not publicly held, then the question of valuation becomes more complicated. Whereas the market value of a publicly held

EXHIBIT 7.4

Price Multiples for Amazon.com and eBay

	Amazon .com	eBay	Sector	S&P 500
P/E ratio (TTM)	NM	128.33	31.55	29.95
Price-to-book ratio (MRQ)	NM	–9.71	4.49	5.21
Price-to-sales ratio (TTM)	2.18	17.90	2.63	3.56
Price-to-cash flow (TTM)	NM	75.61	19.51	21.26
Price-to-free cash flow (TTM)	684.29	60.43	44.05	37.76

TTM: Trailing 12 months

MRQ: Most recent quarter

Source: Multex.com.

company is determinable through stock prices and readily available accounting information, the market value of an entrepreneurial e-business is not readily available. The value of a privately owned Internet company can be measured with methods that are appropriate for entrepreneurial businesses in general. The challenge is to identify "practical, available measures that can be used as proxies for value creation of small and entrepreneurial businesses, which are not publicly traded."[5]

The research of Spivey and McMillan examined the relationship between shareholder return and nonmarket valuation measures in three areas (for small publicly held companies as a proxy for entrepreneurial businesses). Those areas were accounting profitability measures (which includes ratios like return on assets [ROA] and earnings per share [EPS]), cash flow measures, and growth measures. There were relationships between shareholder return and the following measures:

- *Accounting profitability measures*
  - Return on equity $= \dfrac{\text{Income available to common shareholders}}{\text{Average common equity}}$
  - Return on invested capital $= \dfrac{\text{Income after taxes}}{\text{Average total long-term debt, other long-term liabilities, and shareholders' equity}}$
  - Return on assets $= \dfrac{\text{Income after taxes}}{\text{Average total assets}}$
- *Growth measures*
  - Earnings growth = Earnings per share growth rate, as a percentage
  - Sales growth = Sales growth rate, as a percentage

The best measure for companies with negative earnings (a familiar characteristic for Internet businesses) appeared to be sales growth.

EXHIBIT 7.5

Growth Rates and Stock Prices

	Amazon.com	eBay	S&P 500
Sales for most recent quarter versus same quarter one year ago	21.0	59.07	–0.77
Sales—Trailing 12 months versus TTM one year ago	13.9	68.09	2.07
Sales—5-year growth rate	188.05	357.90	12.38
Stock price	18.40	55.784	

Exhibit 7.5 shows growth rates for Amazon.com and eBay and their stock prices in May 2002. It does appear that the market rewards relatively high growth.

The Expected Cash Flow Method versus the Discounted Cash Flow Method

The DCF method discussed earlier involved free cash flows obtained from financial statements and reports of a publicly held company, and discounted with a rate appropriate for the risk in the situation. In general, DCF methods are based on future cash flows, which, of course, are inherently uncertain. That uncertainty helps determine the discount rate used in the traditional cash flow approach.

Financial Accounting Standards Board (FASB) Concepts Statement No. 7 presents an alternative to the traditional cash flow (TCF) approach. The process put forth by the FASB can be used for measurement at initial recognition or fresh-start measurements. It allows for uncertainty, not in the discount rate (as in the traditional method), but in the cash flows. Instead of definite cash flows, the expected cash flow (ECF) approach

IN THE REAL WORLD

Business Valuation

According to Frank Evans, business valuation is more than just review and analysis of financial statements. But it does involve financial calculations, and Evans stresses the importance of cash flow amounts such as the following:

Net Cash Flow to Invested Capital

This amount represents the cash available to interest-bearing creditors and investors after allowing for cash needs to fund capital expenditures and working capital and to pay taxes.

	Net income after taxes	$6,000
+	Tax-adjusted interest expense [1.25 × (1 – 40%)]	750
+	Noncash expense	1,250
–	Capital expenditures	(1,500)
+/–	Change in working capital	(900)
=	Net cash flow to invested capital	$5,600

Net Cash Flow to Equity

This amount represents a proxy for dividends and capital appreciation to common stockholders.

	Net income after taxes	$6,000
+	Noncash expense	1,250
–	Forecasted annual capital expenditures	(1,500)
+/–	Forecasted annual change in working capital	(900)
+/–	Forecasted annual change in long-term debt	150
=	Net cash flow to equity	$5,000

Source: "Tips for the Valuator," *Journal of Accountancy*, March 2000, 35–41.

uses a set of possible cash flows, along with their probabilities. Exhibit 7.6 compares the two methods that one can use to compute a present value. The objective for both methods is to obtain a market value of an asset or liability.

In the TCF approach, the uncertainty affects the discount rate. In the ECF approach, the uncertainty affects the cash flow. One of the uses of the ECF approach is for fresh-start measurements when it is necessary to determine a new carrying value unrelated to whatever amount is currently recorded.

Exhibit 7.7 shows a comparison for a hypothetical example of an asset that will produce a cash flow of $10,000 at the end of year 1 and $10,000 at the end of year 2.

In the ECF approach, there is an 80 percent probability of receiving $10,000, but a 20 percent probability of receiving only $8,000 in the first year. In the second year, the probability of getting $10,000 is down to 70 percent and the probability of receiving only $7,000 is 30 percent. The TCF approach treats the cash flows as contractual but discounts them at 8 percent, which includes the risk-free rate and a premium for the

EXHIBIT 7.6

Discounted Cash Flow Methods

	Traditional Cash Flow Approach	**Expected Cash Flow Approach**
Cash Flows	The contractual or definite cash flow	The expected value of cash flows, weighed by probability
Discount Rate	A rate commensurate with the risk involved	The risk-free rate of interest

EXHIBIT 7.7

Comparison of DCF Methods

	Traditional Cash Flow Approach			Expected Cash Flow Approach				
	Cash Flow	Factor for Discount Rate = 8%	Present Value	Cash Flow	Probability		Factor for Discount Rate = 5%	Present Value
Year 1	$10,000 ×	.9259 =	$ 9,259	$10,000 ×	.80 =	$8,000		
				$ 8,000 ×	.20 =	$1,600		
						$9,600 ×	.9524 =	$ 9,143
Year 2	$10,000 ×	.8573 =	$ 8,573	$10,000 ×	.70 =	$7,000		
				$ 7,000 ×	.30 =	$2,100		
						$9,100 ×	.9070 =	$ 8,254
			$17,832					$17,397

TIPS AND TECHNIQUES

There is a Fortune e-50 Index that was started December 31, 1999, to track the performance of Internet-related companies. The Index contains 50 companies from the following: e-companies, Internet communications companies, Internet hardware companies, and Internet software and services companies. Index statistics provided by *Fortune* can be used to compare the e-50 to the Dow Jones U.S. Total Market Index as well as to individual Internet companies that one might be interested in. In May 2002, some of those Index statistics were:

Index Statistics	Fortune e-50	Dow Jones U.S. Total Market
Hist. 3-yr. EPS growth	59.29%	21.63%
Dividend yield	0.28%	1.44%
Price/Earnings	32.47	21.22
Price/Book	2.12	2.73
Fiscal Year 1 Price/Earnings*	30.33	19.38
Price/Cash flow	15.38	11.07
Return on equity**	6.82%	17.06%

*Price-to-earnings ratio of the previous fiscal year

**A measure of a company's profitability based on earnings per share divided by book value.

Source: *www.Fortune.com* (access *Fortune*'s "lists").

uncertainty of collecting the cash. The ECF approach incorporates the uncertainty when assessing the probability of collection, so it discounts the cash flows at the risk-free rate of 5 percent.

A DCF method that is likely to be used increasingly for fresh-start measurements shows promise for the valuation of assets and liabilities at any point in time, for any purpose, including the valuation of an entrepreneurial business.

Summary

This chapter examined the application of some traditional methods to the valuation of assets or business entities in a context that is still evolving: e-business. Investing in Internet stocks or acquiring Internet start-ups includes elements of decision making that seem to require new approaches because it is all still somewhat unfamiliar. If new valuation measures, like the amount of traffic on a website, are necessary in the short run (since it seems to take some time for Internet businesses to become successful), in the long run profitability is very important. This chapter included methods that have application not only to traditional businesses but also to entrepreneurial and Internet entities. The chapter discussed the discounted cash flow method and the guideline companies method for valuation of a company (and by extension, the company's stock). Also included is a summary of price multiples that can be useful for valuation. Finally, a brief demonstration of a new DCF method, the expected cash flow method, is included to add another tool for valuing an asset, a mix of assets, or an entire entity.

Notes

(Chapters 1 and 4 do not include notes.)

Chapter 2

1. *Statement of Financial Accounting Concepts No. 5*, "Recognition and Measurement in Financial Statements of Business Enterprises," Stamford, CT: Financial Accounting Standards Board, December 1984.

2. Financial Accounting Standards Board. *Current Text 2000/2001 Edition: Accounting Standards as of June 1, 2000.* Volume 1: General Standards. 39749. From FASB Statement 48.

3. Krishna G. Palepu, Victor L. Bernard, and Paul M. Healy, *Introduction to Business Analysis and Valuation.* (Cincinnati, OH: South-Western, 1997).

4. *Id.*

5. *Id.*, pp. 4–5.

Chapter 3

1. Brad Barber, Reuven Lehavy, Maureen McNichols, and Brett Trueman, "Can Investors Profit from the Prophets? Security Analyst Recommendations and Stock Returns," *Journal of Finance* 66.2 (April 2001): 531–563.

2. James K. Glassman, "Faulty Analysis," *The Wall Street Journal*, April 12, 2002.

3. Krishna G. Palepu, Victor L. Bernard, and Paul M. Healy, *Introduction to Business Analysis and Valuation* (Cincinnati, OH: South-Western, 1997) 9–16.

4. Edward I. Altman, "Financial Ratios, Discriminant Analysis and the Prediction of Corporate Bankruptcy," *Journal of Finance* 23 (September 1968), 589–609; Palepu, Bernard, and Healy, pp. 9–17.

Chapter 5

1. See Frances L. Ayres, "Perceptions of Earnings Quality: What Managers Need to Know," *Management Accounting*, March 1994, 27–29.

2. John R. Mills and Jeanne H. Yamamura, "The Power of Cash Flow Ratios," *Journal of Accountancy*, October 1998, 53–61.

3. See *http://aaahq.org/qoe/index.html* for further access to the products of this project.

Chapter 6

1. U. S. Securities and Exchange Commission release, "'Pro Forma' Financial information: Tips for Investors," December 4, 2001.

2. Quotations and all other information about the Trump case are drawn from U.S. Securities and Exchange Commission release, "SEC Brings First Pro Forma Financial Reporting Case: Trump Hotels Charged With Issuing Misleading Earnings Release", 2002–6, January 16, 2002.

3. Joel M. Stern and John Shiely, *The EVA Challenge* (New York: John Wiley & Sons, Inc., 2001), 16. Joel Stern is one of the principals of Stern Stewart. Much of the discussion in this chapter uses *The EVA Challenge* as a primary reference.

4. Arthur Levitt, Jr., "The Money Game," Remarks at the NYU Center for Law and Business, September 28, 1998; available on the SEC Web site at *www.sec.gov*.

5. Stern and Shiely, 16–17.

Chapter 7

1. Bradford Cornell, "Is the Response of Analysts to Information Consistent with Fundamental Valuation? The Case of Intel." *Financial Management* 30.1 (Spring 2001): 131.

2. See Loren Garruto and Oliver Loud, "Taking the Temperature of Health Care Valuations," *Journal of Accountancy* October 2001, 79–93, for additional discussion of the methods.

3. Id.

4. Krishna Palepu, Victor L. Bernard, and Paul M. Healy, *Introduction to Business Analysis and Valuation* (Cincinnati, OH: South-Western, 1997), 7–21.

5. Michael F. Spivey and Jeffrey J. McMillan, "Value Creation and the Entrepreneurial Business," *The Journal of Entrepreneurial Finance and Business Ventures* 1.1, 23–36.

Index